THE CHURCH OF 2020

by Mal Fletcher

'Time and the world do not stand still.
Change is the law of life.
And those who look only to the past or
the present are certain to miss the future.'

John F. Kennedy

'The future starts today, not tomorrow.'

Pope John Paul II

Next Wave International™

Published by Next Wave International™
Visit our website at www.nextwaveonline.com

ISBN 0-9579020-8-5

1. Leadership   2. Future Studies   3. Christian Lifestyle

Unless otherwise stated, Scripture quotations are from the New International Version of the Bible, copyright 1973, 1978 and 1984 by International Bible Society.

Cover Art: Daniel Chattaway, X-Media Design, www.xmedia.com.au
Layout: Next Wave International
Printed in the UK.

Next Wave International™
Post: 155 Regents Park Road,
London, NW1 8BB, UK
office@nextwaveonline.com

and

Next Wave International™
PO Box 106, Reynella S.A., 5161, Australia
gary@nextwaveonline.com

THE CHURCH OF 2020

by Mal Fletcher

Next Wave International™

1

Contemporary Is Not Enough

He was a slave. A nobody. A forced refugee.

He lived without rights in a land that was not his home. Yet he quickly rose through the ranks. He became a trusted advisor, a confidante, to not one but five emperors of an ancient superpower.

His words and the example of his life ultimately changed the destinies of nations and his prophecies about the future of the world are still keenly studied today.

Daniel, or as he came to be known in Babylon, Belteshazzar, was born a Jewish prince in the sixth century BC. As a teenager he was forcibly taken from his home and heritage and transplanted to the Babylon of the great warrior king Nebuchadnezzar.

In the years of Daniel's service, he led two of the kings to faith in God. This is no mean feat in a nation that virtually invented astrology and worship of the stars. Whether they liked him or not, all the kings who knew Daniel respected him. They all agreed: the 'spirit of the gods' was in him (Daniel 5:14).

At the opening of chapter five of the Bible book named after him, Daniel had been out of favour at court for quite a while. Once a highly valued counsellor to Nebuchadnezzar, the greatest of Babylon's kings, Daniel had not been consulted for some time. Instead, he lived in relative obscurity during a time of social upheaval and regime change.

Suddenly, though, he was thrust once more into the royal circle by an unprecedented event: the mysterious writing on the wall.

Looking at how he responded in that moment, we discover a major key to Daniel's enduring influence. We're not told what Daniel was doing in his season of obscurity, not in so many words, yet there are clues to be found in his reply to the king. Daniel had been preparing for his next moment of influence – studying the past and the present so that he could speak into the future.

What It Means To Be Prophetic

Daniel's response to the king in Daniel 5:18-28 reflects the three levels of a truly prophetic life. First, Daniel was clearly a student of the past, as it is seen from God's perspective. In the hands of human beings, all history is propagandized. Historians, even those with the best of motives, will colour events to suit their particular tastes or values. In the end, only God sees history in a truly objective way and it is he who has the final say on history, for history is still 'his story'.

Daniel studied and prayed to understand Babylon's past from the divine perspective. As a result, he knew the background to current events; he saw clearly the foundations on which Babylon's kingdom was resting. Its greatest weakness – perhaps that of all world superpowers – was pride; the arrogance of absolute power (cf. Daniel 5:20-21).

Second, Daniel understood the present from God's perspective. Though the experience of the past should have been instructive to present rulers, it clearly didn't figure in their thinking. It has been said that those who don't learn from the past are doomed to repeat it. Adlai E. Stevenson said that 'we can chart our future clearly and wisely only when we know the path which has led to the present.' Daniel may have been out of the king's sight for a while, but he wasn't completely out of the loop. He had kept his finger on the pulse of current affairs (cf. Daniel 5:22-23).

Being well informed about the past and the present, Daniel was then able to project into the future, under the inspiration of the Holy Spirit. He knew that Babylon's kingdom, in its present guise, could not survive. The current regime was doomed by its own refusal to change or repent (Daniel 5:26-28).

We often think of the Old Testament prophets as super-mystics; men and women who lived on mountain tops, contemplating blades of grass, leaving behind rational thought while they had heavy, other-worldly experiences. In fact, they were very down-to-earth and often scholarly people. They were students of their times who saw themselves as watchers over contemporary generations.

Their knowledge of the real world was an important part of their prophetic role. It wasn't the subject of their message – that came by revelation. But God used their understanding of the times as a canvas on which to paint his vision of the future. They were able to bring God's tomorrow into today. They knew that, as Pope John Paul II much later put it, 'The future starts today, not tomorrow.'

Ahead Of The Times

Like all the prophets of old, Daniel understood three important things. They're as vital for us today as they were for him.

The first is this: for God's people, being contemporary is not an end in itself. To be contemporary literally means to exist at the same time as something or someone else. Churchill and Stalin had little in common, aside from their desire to overcome Hitler. Yet they are called contemporaries, because they lived through the same era in history.

We talk a lot these days about the importance of 'contemporary church' – and so we should. After all, any church should and must 'exist at the same time' as the city it is called to serve. Too often in the past churches have tried to speak to their Babylon without ever learning the Babylonian tongue. Daniel heard from heaven, but he spoke Babylonian.

Contemporary church should not be seen as an end in itself, though. It is a means to an end. The goal is not being contemporary, but becoming prophetic.

We should work to be in touch with the times so that we speak in a way which is ahead of the times. As Christians, we are not all called or gifted to be prophets, which is a good thing – we'd probably drive each other crazy if we were. But collectively, we can speak with a prophetic voice and model prophetic truth to our communities.

To be prophetic is to challenge contemporary values, culture, thinking and behaviour and point the way to something better – the kingdom of God.

God's prophetic people share the present experience of their generation so that they can shape the future destiny of their generation. God reveals his prophetic plans to his people so that they can call their generation into alignment with those plans (cf. Isaiah 43:19).

We cannot be prophetic unless we are contemporary, unless we work to understand the needs, ideas and iconography which have shaped our world. But unless we aim to become prophetic, being contemporary is pointless – we may speak the language fluently, but we'll have nothing unique or fresh to say. Our world will say, 'Why should we listen to you, when you clearly have nothing to offer that we haven't already heard?'

Many Christians fail to influence the future simply because they can't see anything good on the road ahead. For them, the future is a threatening place, filled with bad news. They're looking for the imminent arrival of the antichrist, rather than looking up for Christ's return. The Bible's teaching on eschatology was never given to turn us into hide-under-the-bed escapists. Most often, talk of the end-times in scripture is given in the context of life in the here-and-now. It usually features a challenge to better, or more holy, living.

How should we see the future? Living from a Christian worldview, it is appropriate for us to be wary and cautious, because we know that human beings are fallen. People are capable of great evil, even if they profess to be good. At the same time, we should be hopeful about what people can achieve, for they were created in God's image and still bear the marks of his creativity. We should also be proactive in our own behaviour, taking Jesus at his word

4

when he says that all authority has been given to him and that he has shared his authority with us, empowering us to bring change.

Daniel was heard in Babylon because of the unique revelation he brought. His wisdom reached into a part of the universe Babylonian technology and philosophy could not contact. He brought to men a 'big picture' view of where they were headed – and why.

Influence Is Not What We Think It Is

Daniel also knew that his true influence could not measured by the opinions of those who already agreed with his point of view. Applying this to our time, we can't measure our influence solely by the size of our churches or ministry organisations. Some quite large churches have very little influence in their cities, simply because they gauge their impact by size alone.

The size of our following is usually a *product* of our influence, but it is not the ultimate measure of it. Real influence is measured by how much people *outside* our churches defer to our teaching when *they* have a decision to make.

In a live phone interview for one of our European leadership summits, Pastor Ray McCauley of South Africa asked a pertinent question: 'If your church closed down tomorrow would people in the community care? Or, would they even notice?'

You can apply this at a very personal level, too. Influence means the ability to produce change. Where there is no change, there is no influence. How can we say we're bringing change if the only people who hear us are those who agree with us? We need to aim for respect among those who have little reason to like us, or listen to us.

When a pagan king asks Daniel, the man of God, to unravel the graffiti on a palace wall, that is influence. When Pharaoh asks for Joseph's advice on an emerging national crisis, that's influence.

It's All About The Future

Of all the lessons Daniel had learned during his season of obscurity, the next is perhaps the most significant. True influence is not a product of how well we celebrate the past, or enjoy present. True influence is a result of how well we engage with the future. Daniel drew a line from the past, through the present and into the likely future, based on his understanding of how God works.

Influence is born when we use an informed understanding of the past and the present to help us shape the future. If we don't invent the future, someone else's vision of the future will reinvent us.

In our time, God is once again positioning members of his church in places of great potential influence. Many of them are God's 'sleeper agents'; they're not all that visible yet but, like Daniel, they're ready to shine God's light when the darkness grows deepest.

I have a friend, a well respected pastor, who is running for the presidency of his South American nation. He has often been asked by leading politicians to stand for government, because of the corruption that is rife in the land. After much prayer and consultation, he is now standing for the top job.

Another friend is helping to bring the gospel to sections of the extended European royal family. Behind the scenes, his testimony and his integrity have had an impact on the noble classes. Yet another pastor friend has the ear of the British Prime Minister and is helping to shape various social policies.

A friend in the U.S. was responsible for praying the sinner's prayer with one George W. Bush, back in the days when he was a Texas oilman. And another in South Africa helped to bring racial healing to that nation by working to bring Nelson Mandela, recently released from prison, into face-to-face dialogue with his political opponents.

Of course, God has called each of us to influence – whether or not we mix with 'the great and the good'. In fact, Zambia's former president Kenneth Kaunda once said: 'What a nation needs more than anything else is not a Christian ruler in the palace but a Christian prophet with earshot!'

A City On A Hill

I believe that the most urgent question for *every* Christian is this: what kind of city and nation do you want to be living in ten years from now?

What kind of schools do you want educating your children, or grandchildren? What kind of politicians do you want making the laws by which people live? What kind of media outlets do you want shaping the values of your city? What kind of business practices do you want to see? What views do you want people to have of the family?

More importantly, what kind of future does God have in mind for your city? There's a second part to the question, too. What will you do *now* to set that in motion?

Jesus said that his followers were a 'city set on a hill which cannot be hidden' (Matthew 5:14). We're not meant to be ignored. It's interesting that he said a 'city' and not a club or an organisation. Why did Jesus use that word? I believe it might be because churches can represent, in microcosm, what their cities could look like under God – if people were to return to him and live by Kingdom values.

In most cases, one church working alone doesn't have either the numbers or the resources to change the culture of a city. But it can achieve this by working with like-minded churches across a city. Together they can say to the city: 'If you want to see what family life can be, look at us. If you want an example of how business can be conducted with ethics and justice, look at us. If you want to see good leadership and government, where people willingly work together for positive common goals, follow our lead.'

Faced with the question above, some people, including leaders, will respond: 'What if Jesus returns within the next ten years? Wouldn't that make our planning futile?' If that's true, why does the Bible put so much emphasis on the importance of careful planning (cf. Proverbs 12:3; 16:3; 20:18)? Every Christian should plan as if Jesus won't return for one hundred years, while living as if he might return today!

Church leaders around the world have often asked me, 'How can I bring change to my church, without losing people in the process?' I believe the best answer is this: explain to the people that everything you do is about the future. Ask them whether they're concerned for the spiritual destiny of their children, or grandchildren. Share with them some of the traits and likely achievements of emerging generations.[1] Point out that you're simply trying to build for the future, not just for the present. Reasonable, caring people are usually responsive to that kind of thinking.

I like what my friend, futurist Dr. Tom Sine says: 'Only the Lord Almighty knows fully what the future holds. [Yet] we can use the intelligence the good Lord gave us and a little discernment to ... anticipate some of the change coming at us and find ways to creatively respond before the waves reach us.'[2]

The message of this book is based on 'doing a Daniel'. We need to draw a line from the past, through the present and into the future. We need to ask for God's help to recognize the signs of the times and to identify what kind of churches and ministries we will need to build if we're to truly shape our cities more than they shape us. It's not just about churches and ministries, either. It's also about Christian-run businesses, charities, media organisations, families and more. It's about us as individuals, too.

What will the truly influential church of 2020 look like? What kinds of individuals will influence their world more than it influences them? If present trends continue, what kind of church will truly meet the needs of human beings more than a decade from now? If we know the answer to that – even tentatively – we can begin to build those churches, ministries and lives today. We can prepare in advance, engaging the future and achieving lasting influence.

---

[1] See 'The Future is X', Mal Fletcher (Next Wave International, 2005).
[2] 'Mustard Seed vs. McWorld', Dr. Tom Sine, (Baker Books, 1999), p. 36.

2

Future-Friendly

Christian scholar Kenneth Boulding has said that 'no people, society or organisation can long exist without a compelling image of the better future which calls us forward into tomorrow.' The Christian futures researcher, Dr. Tom Sine, takes a similar line: 'I am convinced that the number one crisis in both society and the church today is a crisis of vision... When I use the term vision, I am not talking about anything spiritual in the clouds. I simply mean the image of the better future that we want for ourselves and those we care about.'[1]

The study of the future has become big business today. Just three decades ago, Alvin Toffler's book *'Future Shock'* became an overnight sensation, because it mixed a well-researched understanding of the present with solid predictions about the future.

Today, futurists charge their corporate clients huge sums of money for the benefit of their research and their prognostications about what is to come. Future study has also become a form of entertainment. Sci-fi movies haven't lost their popular appeal over the years. If anything they've grown in stature as much of today's technology fulfils the seemingly fantastic promises made by early sci-fi writers. Bookstores now feature whole sections devoted to the study of the future.

Futurism has become a highly-paid profession, yet at least one prominent exponent of the art admits that trends are getting harder to predict and read. Dr Patrick Dixon, who has been cited as Europe's leading futurist, says that this is because, 'low probability high impact events strike rapidly and transform our world.'[2]

In a TV interview, I asked Dr. Dixon what a futurist is and why anyone should bother to listen to their predictions. He replied that, actually, we're all futurists to one degree or another. (The only difference, he noted, is that he gets paid quite a lot of money for doing it!)

'We think about the futures of our children,' he said. 'They have more than one future, depending on the choices they make and their circumstances. We wonder about what government will be in power next year. We think about the rate of inflation or what's going to happen to house prices, or whether we'll be able to book a holiday in time. We all think about the future; we are programmed genetically to do that.'

What, I asked, did he say to Christians who say that as only God can see the future there's no point in us trying to predict it?

'I think that's pretty stupid,' he responded. 'If I say to my son, "Well, only God knows the answer to your exam grades in the future, so there's no point in doing any work," that's crazy... Actually we have responsibility. We live in a world of cause and effect. We are products of our own choices. Most people's lives are shaped by the decisions they have made. It's incredibly important that we understand what we can't change and what we could change. We must think responsibly about the things we can't change while also driving what we can change.'

Tom Sine adds: 'let's be clear: only the Lord Almighty knows fully what the future holds. We need to remember that we live in a complex world with an incredible number of variables, a world in which both natural and supernatural forces are at work and over which we have little understanding or control. In spite of that, I am convinced we can use the intelligence the good Lord gave us and a little discernment to read some of the "signs of the times." I believe we can anticipate some of the change coming at us and find ways to creatively respond before the waves reach us.'[3]

Patrick is a committed Christian who spends just one third of his time jetting around the world to speak as a futurist. Most of his time is spent setting up AIDS hospices for the relief of suffering. Tom is also involved in many practical projects which aim to change the future of cities – spiritually, socially and materially. Both men are fine examples of how Christians should respond to the future.

Far from shrinking back in fear of the future, Christians should be the most forward-looking people on earth. In Hebrews

10:38, we're told that God takes no pleasure in people who shrink back in fear, because the just shall live by faith. Faith that pleases God is, then, about reaching forward with courage. As Christians, we are part of a future-minded Kingdom. The kingdom of God is not oriented toward the past; it looks to the future with hope. This hope is not based merely in human optimism, but in a strong awareness of the character and nature of God.

The Scriptures show that God works by faith, relates through love and plans with hope. Every one of these attributes looks not to the stagnant past, but to the dynamic future (cf. Heb. 11:1, Romans 8:25, 1 Cor. 13: 7). Faith, hope and love are not attributes of memory, but of future-mindedness; not of despair but of eager anticipation. When we look forward, we speak God's language.

What's more, we serve a future-minded Lord. Not once in his ministry did Jesus waste time on wistful nostalgia sessions with his disciples. Even in the face of death, he was looking forward (cf. Hebrews 12:2). The role of the church is in part to put 'trainer wheels' on the future. We are meant to give people confidence to ride into tomorrow, knowing that God will look after them if they walk in relationship with Christ.

That's part of our good news message: in Christ the future is bright. 'Let your hopes, not your hurts, shape your future,' says Dr. Robert Schuller. 'The future is as bright as the promises of God,' wrote the Christian world missions pioneer William Carey.

Change Is Constant – Get Used To It

Some people are addicted to change. Novelty, said one writer, has now become the sixth basic human need. Other people fear change. They look at the headlines of today with apprehension and peer over the ledge into tomorrow with terror. Fear has become such a huge issue today that psychology has come up with a new area of study, called terror management theory (TMT). It seeks to explain our reactions to events which shake our sense of certainty and permanence in life – events that terrorize us.

During one of our MasterClass leadership events in the USA, a woman remarked that some of the future technologies I'd described frightened her. I replied that it isn't the technologies we fear so much as the changes they represent. Imagine your great-grandparents had been told about the gadgets you use everyday. No doubt they would have found many of our tools threatening too. Technologies are amoral – it's the change we fear most *and* the abuse of technology.

Whatever you think of change, one thing is sure: the world of 2020 will face an even more rapid wave of change than we experience today. The only thing that's permanent in our world today – aside from the word of God – is transition itself. The immediate future shows no signs of slowing down in that regard.

Let's consider just one area where change is going to increase at a fast click – the area of Internet technology. These changes will not only affect how we communicate, they will impact the very core of our values.

Everything's Changing

By 2020, the computer will no longer be a device sitting on your lap, or your desk; everyday objects and devices will be computerised from the atomic level up using micro- and nano-sensors. Patrick Dixon writes:

> 'We live in a world where there are now more microprocessors than people. The power of PCs has been doubling every 18 months for many years. At that rate it means we will see machines in 2024 with processors that are 10,000 times more powerful than the fastest chips we have today. Expect breakthroughs with nanotechnology within 20 years, allowing chips to shrink massively to microscopic levels.'[4]

Micro-technology is available right now. In 2006 alone, the Gillette company will build ten billion micro-sensors, each no larger than a grain of sand, into its shaving products. Eventually, almost everything we use will have both hardware and software components.

We will use micro-sensors in our clothing. Clothes will 'breathe', with synthetic cloth closing or opening its weave to allow for differences in temperature. Some clothes will wash and dry themselves using built in cleaning micro-units.

Micro-sensors will set your home environmental settings – temperature, humidity and so on. Voice activation will allow you to 'interact' with each room and appliance in your house and with the settings and major functions in your car or on your bicycle. High-end voice activation units, advanced sat-nav technology and intricate accident warning systems will make driving a much more computerized experience than it is today.

Man-Machine Melding

In the past one hundred years, we invited technology into our workplaces, transportation and homes. In this new millennial era we will increasingly invite it into our bodies.

Small processor technology currently allows the manufacture of cochlear implants for hearing loss and retina implants for the site challenged. We can expect to see even smaller microchips melded with human brain matter to form a whole new kind of thinking 'hardware'. These micro-processors will draw their power from the human body itself and even download programs to enhance brain power.

Gradually, aspects of human brain function will be improved to turn the brain into a (very) personal computer. What begins as a response to human ailments will soon become a matter of choice, a lifestyle option, in much the same way that plastic surgery is today. Want a better recall ability? We'll give you a mind-chip. Want a more acute sense of smell? It's a simple surgical procedure – with no after-effects.

We can expect to see the first cyber brain experiments conducted on animals. Cyber-tech will allow digital data to be stored in artificial brains which can be accessed from outside.

In the face of this, the church will need to continue to define what being 'human' means – without reacting in a Luddite fashion to new technologies. Technology is amoral; it is human choice which drives how tools and techniques are applied. Christians will need to do more than speak about new technologies from the outside; they'll need to position themselves at the driving edge of development. For some, this will be a lifetime vocation. They will help ensure that ethical questions are not overlooked in the earliest stages of a new development.

The idea of special creation, where humankind is made in God's image, will need to be voiced loud and clear. The church will need to remind the world that people are not mere machines built to function. Ultra-pragmatism is the great foundation stone of today's technological growth. 'If it can be done,' says ultra-pragmatism, 'it should be done.' The church will need to take seriously its prophetic role; reminding the world that pragmatism, the drive for results, is a good servant but a poor master. It must call the world to use its God-given technological ability to 'subdue the earth' but not to destroy it, to improve life but not to extinguish it.

The church must do all of this in a positive, proactive and engaging way. It must make sure it is known more for what it stands *for* than what it stands *against*.

Le Net and Media Dinosaurs

In 2020, the Internet – or the next incarnation of it – will be more ubiquitous than it is today, allowing access from a much greater number of tools and locations. The word Internet may by then be associated with somewhat outdated technologies, but the principle of interconnectedness, of universal networking, will remain a cornerstone of post-post-modern living.

Virtual reality will be everywhere. Cinemas, theatres and home-entertainment systems will use new forms of 3-D camera and projection to provide a very close approximation to visual reality without headsets and the like. The church of 2020 will use all the technological resources afforded by the continuing information explosion, even building 3-D 'virtual churches', where people can experience church life before committing to face-to-face meetings.

Holographic projection, or the real-world equivalent of this sci-fi dream, will be a day-to-day reality. The projection of miniature or even life-sized versions of real objects or people, in a remote location, will make it possible for business people to 'gather' far from home without leaving their front door. The church of 2020 will make use of this technology for contact with satellite workers – missionaries and church planters, for example. It will also bring in guest speakers from around the world with the click of a button or a simple voice command.

In 1999, a group of US universities worked together to form what they called the 'Abilene network'. Essentially, it offers its members – mainly universities – an advanced alternative to the conventional Internet, with much faster transfer speeds. When established in 1999, the backbone of the network had a capacity of 2.5 gigabits per second. In 2004 an upgrade brought a capacity for 10 gigabits per second. The group will offer 100 gigabit connectivity between every node by the end of 2006. That's fast!

Some futurists foresee the development of an 'Internet iceberg effect'. Internet connections to sensors in household appliances and the like will outnumber human subscriptions. Ninety percent of Internet growth will become invisible, like an iceberg. Everyday tools such as heaters, cookers, toasters, window shades and even toothbrushes may be a linked to the net permanently, for communication with humans or the download of software upgrades.

The *Financial Times* has reported that, 'Homes will be full of addressable processors – you could have thousands of Internet addresses in one house.' We've already seen the early stages of this with the rapid development of WiFi technology and Bluetooth. This has great potential for making our lives easier through automation. Household scanners will record what food items have been consumed – for example, by determining what is in your rubbish bin – and automatically reorder those items from online stores.

At the same time, some people will develop 'net lag'. They will spend so much time on super fast Internet connections that they will expect the rest of life to perform in the same way. As a result, they may grow restless, impatient and unable to stay focused. Other people may develop IDD, Internet Deficit Disorder, a kind of exaggerated Attention Deficit Disorder which results from children using the Internet too much. Used to flitting from one site to another, they may lose some ability to follow a logical, narrative pattern or to follow a path of structured reasoning.

High Touch

At the same time, a counter-trend in society will see a rising hunger for hi-touch in a world of increasing hi-tech. In business, customers will consider human service to be as important a measure of value as price. People will choose one store over another on the basis of the level of human service they're offered.

In the book *'High Tech, High Touch'*, the authors note that: 'Some artists, theologians, scientists, and members of the military, among others, are recognizing and publicly acknowledging that, at its best, technology supports and improves human life, and warning that, at its worst, it alienates, isolates, distorts, and destroys.'[5]

They continue: 'What is high-tech high-touch?... It is embracing technology that preserves our humanness and rejecting technology that intrudes upon it.' Technology, they say, is an integral part of the development of culture, but it must be understood through 'the human lens of play, time, religion, and art.'[6]

The church of 2020 will plan strategically and deliberately programs and spaces which encourage warm human interaction. Church buildings will include spaces where people are able to engage in relaxed conversation and 'real-people-time'. This church will also work against the trend of ever increasing automation of human services. It will use robotic technologies for mundane or overly complex tasks, but will ensure that it keeps a human-to-human interface where this really counts.

So-called Christian TV will be a thing of the distant past. It will have served its purpose, in its time. By 2020, most Christian TV companies will have gone the way of all flesh – except those who have embraced third millennial thinking. In mainstream media, the age of traditional broadcasting – where one or two stations cater for everyone in a society – is already dead. Narrow-casting is now the norm, where stations speak only to clearly defined demographics within the population, as with most cable or satellite outfits.

This, however, is now giving way to video and audio on-demand, via handheld units. Media products are increasingly aimed at smaller and smaller fractions of the overall market. Changes are occurring very quickly today – digital is giving way to hi-definition digital and so on. Expect to see much faster change in the next decade as existing media converge and new media emerge in response to audience demand.

The church of 2020 will use sophisticated communications technology, born out of today's Internet, to build a whole range of programming for different demographics and various end-user media. This church will work to understand both its audience and its chosen media, placing electronic media near the core of its strategic planning. As a result of clever planning and the networking of resources with other churches, it will provide high quality output, 24/7, for a fraction of the cost of today's Christian TV, radio or movies.

The church of 2020 will become its own TV, radio and movie provider all in one. It will do this by releasing those who gifted in this area. It will rely more on a media mission mentality and the work of gifted volunteers than professional media practitioners who have a career but not necessarily a calling or a passion. It will look first for media people who are asking, 'Where can I find an opportunity to serve?' rather than 'How much does it pay?'

Infophobia

The futurist with the quirky name, Faith Popcorn, predicts that as people become more bombarded with information, individuals will start going on 'data fasts'. They will sometimes take a week or a month out of their schedule not to sort through their messages, but to sort out their thinking. 'Don't even try to call me today,' they'll say. 'I'm data-fasting.'[7]

Popcorn also foresees a condition she calls 'infophobia… a psychological syndrome marked by the fear of being incompletely informed… For an infophobic, any statement that begins "Do you know…" results in accelerated heartbeat and panic symptoms.' In an era when we can buy and own more and more, we will have to get used to – ironically – knowing less and less.'[8]

The church of 2020 will not simply need to be aware of the changes which are just around the corner. It will need to be proactive, engaging the future before it happens. Any church of today that wishes to be a player in the world of 2020 will need to begin making that adjustment now. If we're even a little out of the loop now, we can't hope to ever get back in a few years' time.

Many prominent businesses of today will shrink from sight in the next decade or so – because they're trying to use second-millennial thinking to keep up with third-millennial events. The same will be true of many churches. Today they have great resources and a strong presence. In a few years, sadly, they will have passed into relative obscurity as far as their world is concerned.

'Being futurewise is about more than mere predictions,' says Patrick Dixon. 'It is about shaping the future, making history, having contingencies, staying one step ahead.'[9]

There is, of course, a price to pay for long-term influence. My friend Pastor Ray McCauley has been involved in shaping the political and social life of South Africa at some key moments in its transition from apartheid. He has headed up alliances to bring change and started championing the cause of racial integration well before this was part of the mainstream political thinking. Looking back, he openly admits that, 'the more you do for God the more people from different perceptions will attack you. The taller the tree grows the more the wind blows. There's a price to pay for real influence. [But] even those outside the church who attack you will also be taking note of everything you do. You've got to be true to God and you've got to produce fruit, without compromise.'[10]

Want to control the future before it starts to control you? There are some decisions to be made. They can set you up for long-lasting influence in a world of change. Read on…

---

[1] *'Mustard Seed Versus Mcworld'*, Tom Sine, (Baker Books, 1999), p. 36.
[2] *'FutureWise'*, Patrick Dixon (Profile books, 2004), introduction.
[3] Ibid., p. 36.
[4] Patrick Dixon, Op Cit., P. 11.
[5] *'High-Tech, High-Touch'*, John Naisbitt with Nana Naisbitt and Douglas Philips, (Broadway books, 1999), p.3.
[6] Ibid., p.32.
[7] *'Dictionary of the Future'*, Faith Popcorn and Adam Hanft, (Hyperion, 2001), p. 293.
[8] Ibid., p. 294.
[9] Patrick Dixon, Op. Cit.
[10] Interview with Mal Fletcher, 2005. Full interview can be heard at www.nextwaveonline.com.

3

Predictably Surprising

'This is an extraordinary time to be alive, at the start of a new millennium,' writes Patrick Dixon. 'The world is being transformed before our eyes from an emerging industrial revolution and the technological post-war society into something altogether new and different.'

'This millennium will witness the greatest challenges to human survival in human history, and many of them will face us in the early years of its first century. It will also provide us with science and technology beyond our great imaginings, and the greatest shift in values for over 50 years.'[1]

Some of the most exciting yet potentially unsettling changes will come in the areas of information-gathering and the marketing of ideas. According to some marketing experts, most people are already exposed to at least 1600 commercial messages each day. Jeffrey Robinson writes:

> 'In some cases, it could be a lot more, but even if it's only half as many that's still 50 an hour for 16 hours – nearly one per minute. Besides television and radio, there are ads in magazines, newspapers, through the mail, on billboards, in train stations, in trains, at airports, in planes, in supermarkets, in department stores, in museums, at concerts, at sporting events, [and on the Internet and emails]… There are also, now, commercials inside commercials [and product placements in movies].'[2]

This is the world in which we live right now. How much more ad-exposure will we face in the future? Faith Popcorn suggests that we can expect to see an increase in 'brandrogeny', a fusion between the image represented by consumer labels and the lifestyles we lead. Brand names will be used as labels for different demographics in the population – for example, 'MTV types' and those with 'Vogue Attitude'.[3]

Communication companies will squeeze every bit of advertising they can into even the smallest available spaces. A New York Times reporter coined the phrase 'phonespace' to describe the open airtime before phone calls are answered, which could be used for 'sonic branding'.

Gradually, branding will find its way into almost every human activity. We may see, for example, sponsored weddings where couples get deals on the cost of wedding services in exchange for allowing companies to promote their business during the event. Meanwhile, companies in the biotech industry will race each other to develop and brand human body parts, such as artificial blood substitutes. 'The fluids we put into our bodies – from water to beverages – are the most branded items on the planet,' writes Popcorn, 'so it's logical that the fluids *in* our bodies [will] get the same treatment.' [4]

In the face of this, she writes, there will be a 'backlash against the excessive branding of every inch of space and time in our lives [which] will be expressed by a rush to use generic, unbranded products – and raw materials – whenever possible.' She calls this reaction against branding 'brandlash'. [5]

Buzz

Even in today's world, the pushing of products and images is leading to a 'clutter' problem for big business. Coca Cola spent $33 million for the major sponsorship rights to the 1992 Olympics. Despite Coke's huge advertising push, only 12 percent of TV viewers realized that their product was the official drink. Another five percent thought Pepsi was the sponsor!

For individuals, the glut of information is leading to stress, confusion and cynicism. Forced to think on-the-run and to reject ninety percent of what they hear as irrelevant to their lives, people tend to hear only a small part of a message before deciding whether it's for them or not.

Because we're surrounded with so much hype and commercialism, we tend to listen more to word-of-mouth chatter about products and ideas than what advertisers say. Marketers are calling this 'buzz'. Newsweek magazine defined buzz as 'infectious chatter; genuine, street-level excitement about a hot new person, place or thing.'[6]

The world of business is now waking up to the power of buzz. Research has tried to uncover what makes people talk about an idea or concept with their friends. The findings are interesting, especially for a church looking to influence the future.

Buzz, it seems, travels via networks: groups of people who are connected by similar interests or needs. Some people act as buzz creators: they connect more people than average to a new idea. Buzz doesn't just happen, either. It can be deliberately stimulated or encouraged.[7]

How It Works

Looking further into how buzz works, advertisers have found that buzz is easier to create, or encourage, when the product or idea:

i. *Contains something useful:* when the idea gives people results right away.

ii. *Can be previewed:* when people are offered a sneak preview of what the idea can do for them, an opportunity to 'try-before-you-buy'.

iii. *Features a story with a hero or charismatic leader:* when the focal point is a person who has qualities other people want to emulate.

iv. *Can be passed on easily to others:* when give-aways or other incentives make it easy for people to share the idea or product with others.

v. *Delivers what it promises:* when the idea does not over-promise and under-perform.

vi.   *Is not too predictable:* when the product or concept contains something daring and risky.

vii.   *Contains an element of mystery and surprise;* when the product offers a tantalising hint that there may be more to come, as if you need to stay with it to discover the full benefits.

All of the above characteristics apply to the gospel. In fact, in the Bible 'buzz' is simply called 'evangelism'! The spread of the gospel through the first century world, and later through the world, provides a great example of buzz at its most contagious. Which is perhaps why major corporations are now employing what they call 'company evangelists'; people who are paid to create buzz about the company or an idea.

In the next decade or so, the greatest enemy to sharing the Christian message will not be secular humanism, existentialism, materialism, rationalism or liberalism – or any of the plethora of philosophical options on offer. The greatest enemy to communicating the gospel will be predictability. Over the past few years, advertising has changed in many ways. In the midst of all the changes marketing will go through over the next decade or so, one thing remains certain: surprise will continue to be a major ingredient for creating buzz. We are wired to be curious, to want to push the limits of our knowledge. This will matter to a church that seeks influence.

Even today, as soon as you announce yourself a Christian people think they know what you might say on every issue and how you might act on it. Having put you neatly in a box, they feel free to dismiss you out of hand. Yet there's nothing predictable about the life and impact of Jesus Christ. His entire story is packed with surprises.

He's Not Safe

Consider his beginnings. Imagine you have a backstage pass to the angels' performance on the night of Jesus' birth. The official angel choir have been practising down through the aeons of time, making sure they're pitch perfect for the big show on the day of Messiah's birth.

While you watch, word comes through that the big day is here; the angels must take their places in the choir stands. You watch them warming up. It's the most amazing music you've ever heard.

Finally, the curtains part and the angels – thousands of them – start to sing. The sound is amazing, more than you could ever have imagined. But just as they're getting into full swing, they look down. There's a collective gasp of surprise. They've seen what they're singing about: a tiny, helpless human baby lying all scrunched up in an animal's feeding trough. He doesn't look all that comfortable and he's surrounded by an assortment of barnyard animals, a few lowly shepherds and a young girl and her husband. This can't be the One, you sense the angels thinking...

From the very beginning, it's hard to line up the life of Jesus with what you might have expected. Nothing about him was safe or predictable: not his birth, his life, his death and certainly not his resurrection. Jesus did things no one had ever seen done before. He could heal the most awful diseases with just a touch of his hand or a word from his mouth. Sometimes, you didn't even have to be in the same town as Jesus to be healed by him!

Jesus said things no one had ever heard before. Many people who say they have no interest in Jesus quote him often without even knowing it. Such was the impact of his teaching on human history. The Bible says that people were amazed at his miracles and his teaching (Matthew 7:28; 15:31). Most were certainly shocked by the manner of his death.

It's perhaps not really surprising that when Jesus told his disciples about how he would die, Peter took him aside and scolded him. Even today the crucifixion stands as one of the most surprising events in history. Just as Jesus was building a huge following; just as his message was taking hold and his ministry was taking off, he set out on a path to what some might call self-destruction.

Now, there was nothing suicidal about Jesus – he was the most *alive* person anyone had ever encountered. 'In him was life,' wrote the apostle John, 'and that life was the light of men' (John 1:4). Yet he not only *expected* the cross; he *pursued* it. 'No man takes [my life] from me,' he stated. 'I lay it down of my own accord' (John 10:18).

Then there's the resurrection to consider. What can you say? It was a massive shock to all concerned. Even his friends, if they hadn't seen him post-resurrection, would never have believed it. To this day it remains a huge stumbling block for many people when they seriously consider the Christian faith. How can a man rise from the dead? Paul recognised the impact of the resurrection and said that if Christ wasn't raised from death, Christians are 'to be pitied more than all men' (1 Cor. 15:19).

Surprise!

It's not just Jesus' life that's surprising, however. Consider his impact on history as a whole. The Bible claims for him a far greater role than that of prophet or religious leader, as is reflected in these words from Pope John Paul II:

> 'When you wonder about the mystery of yourself, look to Christ, who gives you the meaning of life. When you wonder what it means to be a mature person, look to Christ, who is the fullness of humanity. And when you wonder about your role in the future of the world look to Christ.'

No futurist living in the decades before Christ could ever have accurately predicted the direction of his unique life. Even the prophets of old saw only fragments of the story; pieces which seemed to make little sense until he appeared and put them all together.

The gospel is a surprising message, about a surprising person. God broke through the clutter of humanity's disjointed perceptions and skewed orientation to spring the most unexpected and glittering of all surprises. Through a baby born in a stable, through a man who evicted sickness and made waves stand still, God sprang out at us shouting: 'SURPRISE! I still love you!'

The only thing people should be able to predict about a church it is that it's going to surprise them every time – because it represents Christ. (When was the last time you sprang out at your non-believing friends and shouted: 'Surprise!'?) A church that consciously builds surprise into everything it does will position itself to be heard. The church of 2020 will be buzz central in its community; it will train and release people to be the buzz creators within their circles of influence. It will do this by:

Making The Gospel Visible

This church will refuse to hide its faith, or to shrink from speaking hope and truth in the midst of a despairing, frightened and compromising world. As more and more people tire of living just for material gain or comfort, the church of 2020 will refuse to treat its faith as just another lifestyle option, or another path to personal success. It will no longer try to mirror or simply 'Christianize' the trends of pop-culture, but will become more trend-setting, challenging status quo methods and ideas. It will be bold in its preaching – but positive, emphasizing the 'good news'. It will be a voice for righteousness and holiness, but won't become 'God's police force', trying to impose the gospel on people who reject Christ.

The church of 2020 will also demonstrate how useful faith is on a practical level – in decision-making, relationships, handling money and so on. Wisdom will be in huge demand in 2020 and churches that can show the link between faith and wisdom will have an eager audience.

Celebrating The Hero Of The Story

The church of 2020 will preach Jesus first and foremost. It will talk about issues in the context of how the life and teaching of Jesus affect them. It will respect church history and the opinions and teachings of prominent church leaders past and present, but it will not allow them greater weight than the words of Jesus himself. It will become far less institutional – even less than it is now – and far more radical and, in a sense, simple (though not simplistic).

The person and work of Jesus will feature more in its promotions. It will find ways to communicate Jesus using up-to-date terminology and iconography, without compromising the polemic of his message *or* the often confronting aspects of his person and mission.

Giving People A Preview

The church of 2020 will more than ever seek to provide outward demonstrations of faith's power, at all levels of human need – spiritual, psychological, physical and emotional. While it will not rely on phenomenal revivals to bring growth and influence – revival of the church is only part of God's agenda – it will give supernatural manifestations their rightful place in changing lives, without trying to manufacture them.

Churches will increasingly seek to provide a taste of God's transforming power for people who are not yet born again. They will take the supernatural element of faith 'on the road', doing as Jesus did and going to where the hurting live. The new emphasis on the supernatural will not, however, outweigh other priorities such as practical social action. The church will show the kingdom of God in all its fullness.

Passing It On

The influential church of 2020 will instruct believers in how they too can truly release God's wisdom and power through their lives. What was once called 'Body ministry' will come back to the fore, placing the emphasis not on ministry specialists alone, but on the priesthood of all believers.

The difference between the coming manifestation of this and past versions, will be the presence of effective leadership which channels the energy and gifts of the Body into building something that lasts. Thus the ministry gifts will not be used in an inward-looking way, but as part of the overall, specific mission of one church to its community.

Christians will be encouraged to testify on how the gospel delivers in their lives. Faith will be in the gospel itself, not in the church.

Risky Business

The church of 2020 will demand of its adherents a life of risk, of investing in something larger than oneself. As people seek out ever more challenging, even dangerous, forms of entertainment, the church will provide a clear call to the laying down of one's life for an eternal cause.

The emphasis will be on whole-of-life mission, rather than simply giving *to* mission. Christians will live on the edge, recognizing that God requires more than the tenth, he demands the totality of our lives!

The church's teaching will include how people can use faith principles to enjoy a better life, but its real weight will be on a call to sacrifice. In fact, generous giving will be outweighed by sacrificial giving.

Prosperity will be seen in its prosper context: as the favour of God which must then be invested to 'purchase' influence and honour for his name. The influential church of 2020 will place a high premium on strategic risk-taking and will require that its leaders are personally setting the trend in this regard.

---

1 *'FutureWise'*, Patrick Dixon, (Profile books, 2004), introduction.
2 *'The Manipulators: A Conspiracy to Make Us Buy'*, Jeffrey Robinson, (Simon & Schuster UK, 1998), p. 81.
3 *'Dictionary of the Future'*, Faith Popcorn and Adam Hanfit, (Hyperion, 2001), p. 261.
4 Ibid., pp. 259-260.
5 Ibid., p. 260.
6 Quoted in *'The Anatomy of Buzz: Creating Word-Of-Mouth Marketing'*, Emanuel Rosen, (HarperCollins Business, 2000) p. 263.
7 For more on this, see *'The Anatomy of Buzz'* (Ibid.).

4

Fundamental Not Fundamentalist

In July 2005, the world watched in horror as emergency service personnel began to deal with the aftermath of London's underground bombings. The tube and the wider public transport system, the lifeblood of the city, were brought to a standstill as bombs ripped through several trains and a bus. In the days that followed, the official death count rose to more than fifty.

Since 9/11, one word has come to summarise, in the minds of many, everything that we should fear from the world of terrorism. That word is 'fundamentalism'. Not so long ago, the word simply referred to a belief in the fundamentals of a religious faith. A fundamentalist was someone who accepted the literal interpretation of a religious text and was willing to align his or her life with its moral and spiritual principles.

Today, the word carries an overtone of menace. It conveys small-mindedness, cruelty and injustice. A fundamentalist is now someone who blows up innocent people in a misguided quest to force change upon the world.

Fundamentalists of any stripe are dangerous; whether we're talking about fanatics who act in the name of Islam or so-called Christian activists who blow up abortion clinics or government buildings in cities like Oklahoma.

Terrorism is set to take on new forms in the next decade or so. New terms will come into existence to describe new threats – even if those threats are never realised. 'Repro terrorism' will describe rumours that terrorists have infected water supplies in a way that threatens people's ability to reproduce. 'Agro terrorism' will describe threats to our food supplies through, for example, tampering with genetically modified crops.

Terror entrepreneurs will use low-cost weapons systems and technological attacks to wreak havoc on behalf of the highest bidder. They will form small groups – perhaps even based in families – which will be harder to infiltrate. They will remain free from any affiliation with governments. Offering 'terror services' may well become one of the big competitive industries of the new era.

Distance terrorism will also be a growing threat. The Internet has made it possible for terrorists to cause great damage without ever leaving their homes. In this way, they could remotely cripple whole areas of suburbia, by using our reliance on digital technology against us. Public transport power supplies and safety measures can be disrupted by changing the software programs that drive them. Supplies of food and water in an area can also be damaged by altering computer programs at the source. All of this can be achieved by computer hackers who live on the other side of the world.

As Christians, we do not face the future with fear. 'There is no fear in love,' says 1 John 4:18. 'Perfect love drives out fear.' God has not given us a spirit of timidity, but of power, love and a stable or disciplined mind (2 Tim. 1:7). The point, though, is this: we will need to be careful not to stray into legalism or fundamentalism, which people will associate with religious terrorists.

The church of 2020 *will* emphasize the fundamentals of Christian faith, while steadfastly remaining untainted by fundamentalism.

Sticking To The Fundamentals

In November 2005, Queen Elisabeth made a speech to the Church of England Synod. In it, she talked with heartfelt candour about the 'uniqueness of Christian faith'. She said:

> 'When so much is in flux, when limitless amounts of information, much of it ephemeral, are instantly accessible on demand, there is a renewed hunger for that which endures and gives meaning.'

'The Christian Church can speak uniquely to that need, for at the heart of our faith stands the conviction that all people, irrespective of race, background or circumstances, can find lasting significance and purpose in the Gospel of Jesus Christ.'

Reflecting on the Queen's comments, the editorial of a major British newspaper made the following observation: 'As the Queen implied yesterday, it is, paradoxically, Britain's Christian particularism that protects the multitude of other religions that flourish here... The protection of minorities is best served by a common respect for the historic culture of the country.'

Even in an age of cynicism and criticism of Christian institutions – some of it warranted – many people are looking to the Christian church to actually stand for something. Many in the community – even newspaper editors, it seems – are hoping that the church might provide a solid and strong voice to a culture in which political correctness has produced only more confusion and fragmentation.

Political correctness is politeness turned sour. The courtesy and tolerance of which we boast in today's avowedly multi-ethnic Western nations, is in many ways a by-product of Christian faith.

We are not children of nothing: our thought and values sprang from and are still influenced by our cultural parentage. T. S. Eliott, the celebrated poet, noted the close historical link between the Christian faith and worldview and European civilisation generally:

'The dominant feature in creating a common culture between peoples, each of which has its own distinctive culture, is religion.'

'I am talking about the common tradition of Christianity which has made Europe what it is and about the common cultural elements which this common Christianity has brought with it. It is in Christianity that our arts have developed; it is in Christianity that the laws of Europe – until recently – have been rooted. It is

*against a background of Christianity that all our thought
has significance.'[1]*

Historian Norman Davies writes: 'Most [scholars of
medieval history] would agree that the unifying feature of the
mediaeval world is to be found in organised Christianity.' Most
Europeans up to the medieval period, he writes, would have seen
themselves as Christians living in a Christian part of the world.[2]

Even during the Enlightenment, when Christianity was
under heavy attack, it continued to play a central role. Voltaire, who
launched vicious attacks on established religion and what he saw as
its empty superstition, nevertheless sprang to defend the existence
of God.

Reflecting on the sky at night, he said, 'One would have to
be blind not to be dazzled by this sight; one would have to be stupid
not to recognise its author; one would have to be mad not to
worship him.' He went on to say, wittily, 'If God did not exist, he
would have to be invented.'

Many of the Enlightenment's greatest philosophers, still
revered as giants of European thought, could never have emerged
had there been no Christian faith. The roots of their philosophies –
and the passion of their commitment to them – often sprang from a
desire to denounce the dead, institutional religion which had so
infected the Christian church. Eliott puts it succinctly: 'Only a
Christian culture could have produced a Voltaire or a Nietzsche.'

What is does the future hold for the West? One thing, at
least, is sure. There can be no Western culture without reference to
its 'cult': the underlying religious belief which in one way or another
has   driven   its   development   for   so   long.

The church of 2020 will stick to – in some cases, return to
– the fundamentals of its faith, flying in the face of political
correctness. It will boldly, but positively, announce that all roads do
not ultimately lead to the same destination. It will openly challenge
the claim that it's alright to believe something is true, as long as you
don't insist it is *the truth* for everybody. It will preach and model the

fundamentals of its faith, without, in the words of Winkie Pratney, 'cant, cloud or compromise'.[3]

Where's The Difference?

What is the difference between a church of fundamentals and the world of fundamentalism? Fundamentalism puts dogma or creed above people. This is something Jesus never did. He had more problems dealing with the hyper-religious Pharisees and Sadducees than he did with common people, or even die-hard social outcasts.

The Pharisees saw themselves as the divinely appointed protectors of the Mosaic Law. Ostensibly to stop Israelis accidentally breaking the Law of Moses – which was hard to do, given that the Law was so clear and detailed – the Pharisees invented a heavy code of extra laws.

Without diluting it, Jesus boiled the entire body of Old Testament law down into two sentences. He taught that the two greatest moral mandates from God are that we love him with all that we have and are and that we love our neighbour as ourselves (Matthew 22:37-40).

Jesus refused to worship a creed or dogma. He embraced the Law of Moses – without the Pharisaic appendices. In fact, he said that he came not to destroy the law but to fulfil its requirements on our behalf (Matthew 5:17). The Greek terms he used here suggest the work of an accountant who balances his books by personally making up the debt side of the table. Jesus made up our debt when it comes to Old Testament law. Besides, taught Paul, the law was really only our childhood tutor, keeping us in line until Jesus arrived and brought us his gospel (Galatians 3:24).

Jesus always claimed that the law had been given for the benefit of people, rather than for their harm. This is summed up in Mark 2:27: 'The Sabbath was made for [because of, for the sake of] man; not man for the Sabbath'. Divine law was given for our enrichment, not our enslavement.

To most people today, 'moral law' means arbitrary rules applied to prevent people expressing themselves. In the Bible, God's moral principles are value-adding. What's the most well-known body of moral law in the Bible? The Ten Commandments (cf. Exodus 20 and Deut. 5). Yet if you study these commands, you see that they were originally intended to be life-enlarging, not life-enslaving.

Even today, living by the principles behind these laws adds value to our lives. Having no other gods before God adds true worship to our lives. Making no idols adds clear vision to our lives. Not misusing God's name adds reverence; keeping the Lord's Day adds balance and honouring our father and mother adds honour. Refusing to kill adds respect for life; refusing to commit adultery adds covenant loyalty; refusing to steal adds trustworthiness.

Refusing to testify falsely against our neighbour adds integrity to our lives and refusing to covet adds contentment. In the Bible, God's moral law is *descriptive* before it is proscriptive: it marks out the boundaries of a healthy and rich life.

True faith is never destructive; it releases, it does not seek to bind; it ennobles, it does not degrade. You can be fundamental in faith, without taking on the heavy scowl of fundamentalism.

The church of 2020 will put people above dogma, by showing how living within God's moral principles – in the power of grace – elevates day-to-day life.

Alienation In The City

In the city of the near future, alienation will threaten social harmony in ever increasing ways. In the next decade or so, some social barriers will come down but others will spring up in their place. The clash of civilizations will continue, contributing to terrorism.

Political correctness in the West will further weaken traditional, largely Christian-based cultures, leaving the door to influence wide open for less tolerant, more militant groups. Gradually, a counter-trend will emerge, where more and more non-Christian voices will call for a return to Christian-based cultural values.

On the international scale, the face of warfare will change rapidly. In the twentieth century, wars were fought over ideology, territory or access to natural resources. In the next decade or so, wars will be fought over access to information and know-how. One nation will wage war with another because it doesn't want to get left behind in the 'knowledge race'.

Today, huge biotech and chemical companies are buying up the patents on seeds and superior strains of crops. There is already a strong possibility that they may one day own more than half the world's staple food supplies. Nations may well go to war to prevent this or to correct the imbalance.

Meanwhile, the arms race will continue to dominate international relations, with more nations trying to join the 'nuke-family'. Those who cannot afford this option will look to bio-chemical or perhaps hi-tech, lower-cost nano-weaponry. Others will settle for so-called 'dirty bombs', 'suitcase bombs', or electronic pulse technology which will allow protagonists to wipe out electronic services over a wide area.

In this very unsettled and volatile environment, socially concerned people will seek out leaders and groups who practice reconciliation. They will search for the next Martin Luther King, Mother Teresa or Nelson Mandela. In answer to this, the church of 2020 will boldly announce its mandate of reconciliation (2 Cor. 5:18). Armed with a strong sense of its worldview, the church will teach that alienation is not just a result of human culture – it is an issue of human nature. There are many cultural reasons for alienation, but alienation is essentially sin's first consequence.

Sin cuts us off from the God who made us, the people whom God gave us and the purpose God has for us. Carrying this message, the church of 2020 will set out to break down walls of alienation wherever they are found. It will begin this process in-house, refusing to let church culture alienate those who do not understand or 'own' it.

The Less Clicks The Better

The Internet, as it is today, touches so many areas of our lives. We buy, sell, bank, chat and are entertained on the net. Twenty years ago, Internet technology was the preserve of a few military strategists at the Pentagon and egghead scientists in laboratories such as those at CERN.

Today, there more than two million known commercial websites in cyberspace and the number is growing fast. In November 2005, just under 1 billion people – almost one sixth of the world's population – were accessing the Internet on a regular basis.

We've already considered some of the changes coming with new generation Internet tools. But whatever the future holds for the Internet, we can say one thing with confidence. It will play an even greater role in our lives than it does today. The Internet will become much more an entertainment medium as it merges with other media such as TV and movies. Yet it will remain at least in part a service-based medium. People will continue to go to the net to find answers to questions, problems or needs.

To provide a solid service, today's most successful websites are designed for ease of movement. The demand for effortless use will grow as technology makes this more possible. Top net designers will continue to use relatively simple interfaces which require little from the user, while offering a great experience. Their motto will continue to be 'the less clicks the better': the less people actually have to do to access benefits or services, the better.

The church of 2020 will carry the same motto – the less clicks the better. It will understand how to move people around quickly. It will help people to get from where they are to where God might like them to be, with as few obstacles (or 'clicks') as possible.

No Stairway To Heaven

Being fundamental, the church of 2020 *will* make a strong call to discipleship. But it will seek to change in people only what God wants changed, the way God wants to change it. Anything else is Pharisaic legalism.

The church of 2020 will also engage much more positively with its opponents in society, creating the grounds for dialogue and debate. The motivation will not be to compromise on essential matters, but to offer a proactive demonstration of Christ's love for all. This church will willingly visit turf that is not its own.

This church will not back away from big issues or hide within a comfortable Christian sub-culture. It will see itself as having responsibility for the state of its city, rather than simply the condition of its members.

The church of 2020 will recognise that it has an internal culture and celebrate – but not worship – it. Leadership is not primarily about building organisations but creating cultures. To lead any group of people well you must first create a new sense of what is healthy, acceptable and normal thinking and behaviour in that group. A healthy culture is fundamental to a strong sense of identity, which leads to growth. Here are ten facts about group and church cultures:

i.   *The group that has the strongest culture will become the leading voice in a society.* Why do small lobby groups often exercise a level of influence in society that is way out of proportion to their size? Because they have developed a strong sense of identity and purpose based around their values and culture.

ii. *Whoever defines the culture rules the group.* If someone other than the leader is shaping the culture, cues for the group will be coming from all the wrong places.

iii. *The strongest convictions will shape the culture.* Leaders must have deeply felt convictions and proven values which are born out of personal revelation and practical experience.

iv. *Cultures tend to attract people of their own kind.* If you want people of character, purpose, vision and excellence in your church, business or organisation, you need to create a culture where these things are promoted and celebrated.

v.   *Cultures must be maintained.* Having set the culture – which can take two to three years in a new church or organisation – you must work to keep it alive. Maintain the momentum by exposing your team to like-minded, successful people from outside your organisation.[4]

vi.   *People, left to their own devices, will often return to their old cultures.* You must provide incentives and demonstrate results so that people will not give in to the pressures of entropy.

vii. *Culture brings people together around common ideals, not just common tasks.* A strong culture can never be built around simply performing a task or meeting a goal. It must go deeper than that, to fulfil a common cause and meet a shared aspiration within people's hearts.

viii. *The mix of weak organisation/strong culture can grow.* The mix of weak culture/strong organisation won't survive! In a church, even if you have a Sunday of relatively 'weak' services, you will still grow if your culture is strong.

ix.   *Healthy church culture builds access ramps not stairways to heaven.*

x.   *Church culture is a good servant and a poor master.* Culture becomes a problem only when we forget that we have one – when we expect everyone outside to automatically understand why we believe and behave as we do.

My friend Dr. Jerry Savelle, the noted Bible teacher, has said that he was kept from Christ for years because of the negative and uninspiring behaviour of some Christians. Now he is one of the most effective exponents of faith teaching. If we're not very careful our church culture becomes a series of steps or stairs which people must negotiate if they're to gain access to Christian truth. Our culture can close the door of the Kingdom in people's faces. This happens only when leaders look inward, measuring their effectiveness against that of other churches, rather than by how they're seen in the wider community.

The church of 2020 will recognise that Christians are not called to build a 'stairway to heaven', but an access ramp. It will try to remove obstacles for the 'spiritually challenged' – those who want entry but don't have a religious background. The church of 2020 will constantly ask the 'why' question, as if there must be a good reason for everything it does – even the little things. As a result, it will spend much less time on the 'what', 'how' and 'how much' questions.

Plans are built on strategies, which are founded on vision – and vision is shaped by values and motivations. When values and vision are clearly defined, the reasons for doing something are clear and those motivations lead to certain actions. So, the 'what-to-do' becomes clear.

When values and vision are well thought out and clearly defined, finding practical ways to carry them through is relatively easy. And when values and vision are strongly felt, people are willing to pay *any* price to fulfil them; no cost will dissuade them.

---

[1] Quoted in *'Europe: A History'*, by Norman Davies, (Pimlico, 1996), p. 9.

[2] Ibid, p. 292.

[3] From the introduction to *'Burning Questions'*, Mal Fletcher, (Nelson-Word, 1994).

[4] For more on church culture, see www.s4leadership.com.

5

The Spirit of Jubilee

In July 2005, more than 200,000 people joined to together in London's Hyde Park for a unique event called *Live 8*.

They came from all walks of life and from across the ethnic and generational divides not just to enjoy an historic musical celebration, but to collectively make a statement. They were saying: 'We believe that poverty, especially in Africa, can be ended and we want to be a part of achieving that.'

Sir Bob Geldof, Bono of U2 and a host of other celebs and political heavyweights have lately joined forces to highlight the issue of world poverty. We can expect this trend to continue and gather momentum.

We will see more Hollywood stars and pop-idols travelling the world to represent causes. Some will even put their careers on hold to serve, driven by a deep spiritual desire to make a change in the world. This will be especially true as the Millennial generation comes to prominence, bringing their civic-minded, institution-building and global perspective to the fore.

Some will question the motives of celebrities who get involved in foreign aid and debt-cancellation. The church of 2020, though, will thank God for their efforts, even if these people are unaware of the true source of their altruism.

He may not always get the credit for it, but it was the God of the Bible who initiated the concepts of social justice, world-scale aid programs, equitable trade and debt cancellation. Much of the ministry of the Old Testament prophets involved calling nations to just treatment of the poor. In fact, God made clear that he wants more than justice for the poverty-stricken; he wants mercy. He also provided a model for how a society might promote this – he called it Jubilee.

If you listen to the discussion surrounding campaigns like Make Poverty History, you will hear much that's reminiscent of Jubilee (in part because the campaign started among Christians and was called 'Jubilee 2000').

Reflecting on the need in our time, Bono says: 'Holding the children to ransom for the mistakes of the grandparents, that's a justice issue. Or not letting the poorest of the poor put their products on our shelves while advertising the free market, that's a justice issue to me. These things are rooted in my study of the scriptures.'[1]

In Old Testament times, God ordained that every fiftieth year should be, as Jesus later put it, 'the year of the Lord's favour'.

In that one year, all debts in Israel were to be cancelled. People who had lost land through debt could have it returned to them. Those who were living in debtors' prisons were to be set free (Leviticus 25:10-55). (Debt was the most common reason for imprisonment in those days, so this was especially attractive.)

Jubilee meant giving the 'little guy' a chance to climb out from under his mountain of debt. It was also aimed at correcting the unfair advantage which is present in so many debt situations. It was not so much about simple charity – or aid – as promoting a fresh opportunity for self-sufficiency.

The year of Jubilee wasn't always kept in Israel, yet it still stands as a reminder of how God acts and thinks. He is generous and merciful and expects us to be the same (cf. Matthew 18:23-35).

Perhaps Jesus had in mind people like those living in Africa's poorest regions when, right at the start of his mission, he borrowed from Isaiah 61 to make this announcement: 'The Spirit of the Lord is with me. He has anointed me to tell the Good News to the poor. He has sent me to announce forgiveness to the prisoners of sin and the restoring of sight to the blind, to forgive those who have been shattered by sin, to announce [Jubilee] the year of the Lord's favour' (Luke 4:18).

The Year Of God's Favour

A few years back I was speaking for a major ministry in the USA. As I arrived at the airport, fresh from a speaking tour in Europe, I was greeted by a well dressed young man who took me to his car. I had to look twice. It was the biggest limo I had ever seen; the mother of all limousines. The ministry had provided it for me, as it did for all of its guest speakers. Some Christians might say a preacher should think twice before stepping into a car like that. Although I'm looked after quite well when I travel (thanks to all my hosts out there!), I haven't been driven around in limo's too often, so I didn't do too much second-thinking.

Inside, it was huge. If you're into golf, you could have played the entire eighteenth hole back to the clubhouse right there in the back of that car. As we drove away, I thought about how much I enjoyed this kind of special treatment. It certainly isn't my everyday experience, not by a long way, but it was great when it happened.

When Jesus spoke about 'the Lord's favour', what did he mean? He meant something like what I experienced in the back of that limo – only on a much bigger and more meaningful scale. God's favour is his special treatment of those who love and obey him. He places his smile on people who seek to do his will; it looks like a spotlight out of heaven, separating them from others.

No, Christianity is not a life of endless bliss and no nasty surprises. In fact, sometimes being a Christian can *cause* you problems (cf. Luke 12:49-53). Yet even in the midst of those tough times, there is an open heaven experience, the unseen hand of God protecting and guiding our steps. And there is a profound sense that, even if our feelings dictate otherwise, God has not left us (Matthew 5:11, Hebrews 13:5).

Jesus Christ came to extend the spirit of Jubilee, or God's 'special treatment', to people of *every* country and people on earth. Under his ministry, Jubilee went from being a concept given to one nation and became a potential blessing to all nations.

What The World Needs Now...

Our world certainly needs Jubilee. According to the New York Times, 358 billionaires now control assets greater than the combined incomes of countries that represent 45 percent of the world's population. Ours may be an age of unprecedented opportunity in many ways, but the chance to gain real wealth is restricted to a very small percentage of the world's people.

The gap between the haves and have-nots is expanding, even in developed countries. Some forecasters foresee the development of a permanent underclass in even the most liberal economies of the world, such as the USA.

Meanwhile, a new form of apartheid is on the horizon, based not around economics but knowledge.

'The world will divide into information haves and information have-nots,' writes Patrick Dixon. 'The privileged majority will accelerate... leaving a digital underclass far behind... Every nation will contain both communities and a nation's future prosperity will be determined by the proportion of haves and have-nots, something which will change fast in many poorer nations...'[2]

The church of 2020 will be a place where people find the spirit of Jubilee alive and well. It will be expressed not just in generous giving, but in the promotion of others to new levels of opportunity in every aspect of life. Generosity, in fact, will give way to real sacrifice, where Christians give more than their money – they will lay down time, energy, ambition and personal goals to help lift others at home and abroad. At a financial level, they will give expecting accountability from organisations charged with distribution. But they will not seek to control the outcomes or the recipients of their giving.

Individual Christians may not have the power to grant the nations of the world a year of Jubilee, or to single-handedly bring balance to a world of advantage and disadvantage. But in the church of 2020, Christians will be well informed about the most pressing problems and the most do-able solutions. Providing the means of self-sufficiency and a new start to people who have never known favour will be a core part of the church's vision and strategy.

Individual Christians can make a difference to issues of need by adopting a Jubilee lifestyle. Whilst not the church's primary motive, doing this will position the church for influence in a society which will increasingly hunger to see Jubilee in action. The Jubilee lifestyle is characterised by a series of choices.

Living Simply

God does not call every Christian to take a Franciscan vow of personal poverty. The problem of poverty is not solved by more poverty. But God does require that we move away from a life of excessive luxury and ease. In a land where we are blessed with so much, this can only happen by choice.

I would rather live a relatively comfortable life than a harshly uncomfortable one. Yet excessive comfort kills the one kind of poverty the Bible actually applauds, which is poverty of spirit. Jesus said: 'Blessed are the poor in spirit...' (Matthew 5:3). That word 'blessed' can be translated: 'happy, fortunate and to be envied'. God is obviously pleased with this kind of poverty.

Poverty of spirit is the certain knowledge that without God you would have nothing. That all your possessions are worthless in comparison with knowing him. That money may be able to buy temporary happiness, but it certainly can't buy everlasting joy.

Excessive comfort and easy living encourage self-sufficient pride, dulling our spiritual senses. They breed materialistic thinking, to the point where things start to 'own' us.

In 1 Corinthians 9:26-27, Paul makes this interesting statement: 'I don't run without a goal. And I don't box by beating my fists in the air. I keep my body under control and make it my slave, so I won't lose out after telling the good news to others' (Contemporary English Version). The Greek language of the original is even more compelling. In it Paul says something like this: 'I tease and annoy my body until it gives in; I subdue my desires until they comply.' He adds: 'I am a slave-driver to my own body'.

They're tough words, but Paul knows that life is not about lifestyle and material comfort. Jesus put it this way: 'Be careful to guard yourselves from every kind of greed. Life is not about having a lot of material possessions' (Luke 12:15).

Our popular culture would re-write Paul's words this way: 'I make a lot of movement, but don't really hit anything. I have activity but not much achievement. My body keeps *me* under control, until I'm a slave to what *it* wants, when it wants it.'

Jubilee lifestyle begins with making deliberate choices every so often which 'tease' or 'annoy' our physical tastes, so that our actions and values comply with higher goals. For some of us, this might mean fasting now and again. Or perhaps fasting from TV, or the Internet, or some other pleasurable activity. For others it may mean passing our favourite shopping mall or department store and keeping the credit card firmly in the wallet or purse!

Tom Sine comments: 'We cannot practise biblical discipleship over the top of the acquisitiveness, materialism, individualism, and consumerism of modern culture and wind up with anything that bears much resemblance to Jesus...'[3]

Jubilee is not about living with a poverty mindset. Far from it: it calls for the use of abundant, God-given resources to help lift and liberate others. Jubilee begins, though, with the active pursuit of self-control, so that we remind ourselves of our higher, kingdom priorities *and* free up practical resources, such as time and money, for other purposes. The church of 2020 will practice this in a very positive and joyful way.

Being Content

The story of Job is a riches-to-rags-back-to-riches story. He lost everything in one day, through no fault of his own. It was *really* 'one of those days'. Job might have wished he hadn't got out of bed in the morning. All he was left with were a few friends of the kind that make you prefer your enemies.

What was Job's first response? Did he break out the Muddy Waters albums and sing the blues? Did he moan along with Eric Clapton, that 'nobody loves you when you're down and out'? Actually, he said something quite remarkable: 'Naked I came from my mother's womb, and naked I will depart. The Lord gave and the Lord has taken away; may the name of the Lord be praised' (Job 1:21).

Some commentators have said that this is a statement of doubt. After all, it wasn't God who did this to him, but the devil. I think, though, that Job's is a statement of extraordinary faith. Think about it. Which is easier to say, in times of extreme difficulty: 'Well, that's it for me; my best days are behind me; God has forgotten me and the devil is at the wheel'? Or, 'I don't know how and I can't see where, but I know that somehow, somewhere my God is still in control of my destiny'?

Job was genuinely hurting, but he'd learned the power of contentment. Contrary to popular belief, contentment doesn't mean lying down and taking whatever life dishes up to you. If you read Job's full story you'll find he could be pretty feisty at times. He was no pushover. Contentment means being grateful for what you still have, when the natural tendency is to focus on what you've lost or to covet what belongs to someone else.

The church of 2020 will be able to release resources because individual members will practice contentment. They will not be into hoarding possessions for the mythical 'rainy day'; nor will they be driven by a desire to own what others do just for the sake of appearances. Most of them will not be poor by the standards of their society and they will be wise with their money. But their major priority will be on serving God rather than mammon. In other words, they will be stewards not 'storers'.

Giving Dangerously

In Luke 6, Jesus told us that it's no credit to us if we lend only to those from whom we can expect a return. Neither is there anything laudable about loving only those who love us. Kingdom living is about going beyond what is expected. It's about rising above the ordinary to achieve the extraordinary; it means going past the mundane to spring a surprise. It means prophetically challenging the status quo and pointing the way to something better. This applies to our giving of time and money as much as anything else.

The church of 2020 will give dangerously by going beyond the call of duty in its support of worthy aid organisations and people. It will not be motivated to give simply by the latest headlines. Its giving will be more strategic than that, with a clear long-term agenda and clearly measurable goals. For this church, giving to aid and development programs will be as much a part of its central vision and strategy as are preaching and disciple-making.

Giving dangerously also involves giving when it goes on costing us. It is relatively easy to give something once, in an offering for example, but it is much more challenging to give something today and still feel the cost tomorrow. The church of 2020 will promote sacrifice rather than simple generosity. This church will ask of its members: 'what can you responsibly give today that will still cost you in one month or one year from now?' It will also positively model and promote the idea that to give one's time is often as important as donating one's money.

Time has been called the currency of the future. Even today, time is as important as money for many people. When we apply for a job, we no longer ask only about the wage on offer. We ask questions about time, too: 'How many holidays will I get? Will I be able to work flexi-hours? What is the time allowed for paternity or maternity leave?'

The church of 2020 will receive offerings which have a money *and* a time component. People will be able to pledge their time resource at the same time as they invest their money. For some members who have little to give financially, it will feel rewarding to donate time. Even the wealthiest members will find special satisfaction in putting their shoulder to the wheel, as this brings a whole new sense of satisfaction and a passion for Jubilee living.

The church of 2020 will promote Jubilee on every level — for the individual, for the local community, for the nation and for far-flung regions of the world. It won't stop preaching or evangelising, for spiritual release is the cornerstone of real Jubilee. But it will augment these with practical works to back up or, more often, precede the message.

It won't give simply to be seen giving or because other churches are giving. This church will place giving aid and supporting – or initiating – redevelopment programs right at the heart of its own mandate, because it is part of God's holistic plan and reflects his heart for humanity.

On the other hand, it will not be afraid to promote its social activities in the press and media. It will see this not as an opportunity for self-promotion, but to raise awareness of the full scope of the gospel. Promoting positive Christian action makes *God* famous!

The church of 2020 will invest in programs which do more than throw money at problems. It will seek out projects that invest for long-term change. This church will form alliances, knowing that it cannot achieve everything alone; it won't simply invest in projects that have its name on them.

This church will link with organisations whose aim is to promote self-sufficiency among the impoverished. It will take more joy in seeing people produce for themselves than having people forever reliant upon its help. It will not give in a fleeting way, supporting projects only for a month or two. It will invest even when results are slow to come, believing that sowing is essential to eventual reaping. And when projects *are* starting to produce the desired results it will shift *some* resources to help build programs in other places.

Taking It Beyond Money

The spirit of Jubilee is not just about financial conditions. Jesus showed that Jubilee and the opportunity for a second chance must be extended to all levels of human need. His teaching, including its extensive instruction on money, was aggressively backed with the working of miracles and signs – most often involving healing. He promised that the same signs would follow those who believe in him.

Like Jesus, the church of 2020 will extend the Jubilee spirit to cover human health. The increase in world population, combined with the high mobility brought about by world travel, have already exposed us to a growing risk of global epidemic. We are already seeing rapidly changing viruses emerge in different parts of the world.

AIDS is, of course, the most tragic example of a viral strain which began its life among animals and then mutated to attack human beings. Patrick Dixon, futurist and physician, writes: '[With AIDS] we are seeing one new infection every 15 seconds... Ninety percent of all new infection is among heterosexuals. In 1996 more people died of AIDS in the US than in the entire ten year Vietnam war.'[4]

In 1918-1919 Spanish flu swept the world. It wiped out 30 million people. SARS (severe atypical respiratory syndrome) appeared in 2003 and sent shock waves around the world. In the end, it didn't affect more than a small number of people but new viruses continue to emerge. Scientists have long warned us that another virulent strain of flu could emerge at any time. Dixon continues: 'Every time a new person is infected [with a virus] there is a small risk of a significant mutation... We have no medical protection against viral plague, no equivalent of penicillin for viruses...'[5]

By 2020, though, finding cures for fast-mutating diseases may become a matter of human survival. In the face of this, extensive research, into gene technology among other things, will aim to find life-saving antiviral treatments. This kind of research will become bigger business than ever, leading to great breakthroughs and, inevitably, to great abuses of corporate power. The church of 2020 will also make its voice heard on issues such as this, calling and modelling a righteous use of human skills and medicines.

The church of 2020 will believe in and for divine healing. People with sicknesses – even of the worst kind – will be welcomed. The church will place great emphasis on prayer as the medium for miracles. Being an agent of divine healing will not be the sole prerogative of gifted 'expert practitioners', but the right of every Christian who will stand together with others in faith. Those with a special manifestation of this gift will equip the Body as a whole to minister healing in a humble but authoritative way.

We can expect a trend where more medical treatments are offered by health professionals outside the traditional doctor's surgery or hospital. Already in nations like Britain some treatments are offered in small clinics within railway stations and pharmacies, to relieve the pressure on hospitals. In line with this, many churches will run professionally staffed clinics. The church of 2020 will also be involved in providing places of comfort, restoration and assistance for people who are undergoing medical treatment and need practical support. Churches will, often in alliance with other community groups, provide local hospices. These will develop positive links with state-run hospitals.

The church of 2020 will go one step further, bringing back to church life a belief in the power of natural restoratives. It will not become a dispensary for pseudo-scientific 'cures', but a place where there is emphasis on proper diet, exercise and other factors which promote ongoing health. This church will carry the spirit of John Wesley and other early evangelists who practiced and taught on the power of herbal remedies and healthy lifestyle choices.

As the Boomer generation grows old, this so-called 'youth generation' will refuse to lie down and die. Already, Boomers are spending more than any previous group on plastic surgery and other enhancement techniques including hormonal treatments and a plethora of nutritional supplements. There are 77 million Boomers in the US alone and they will continue to reach for the illusive nectar of everlasting youth. Health will be a huge issue for them.

The church of 2020 will offer Boomers health guidance, prayer for healing and new levels of support for the aged. Along with the opportunity to invest their latter years in kingdom activity, leading to peace of mind.

In its giving and its care for the sick, the church of 2020 will pioneer a new expression of Jubilee. It will show that what the crowds at Live 8 longed to see is actually alive and well, week by week, in the church of Jesus Christ.

[1] *'Bono on Bono: Conversations with Michka Assayas'*, (Hodder and Stoughton, 2005) p. 123.
[2] *'FutureWise'*, Patrick Dixon, (Profile books, 2004), p. 22.
[3] *'Mustard Seed Versus Mcworld'*, Tom Sine, (Baker Books, 1999), p. 162.
[4] Patrick Dixon, Op. Cit., p. 113.
[5] Patrick Dixon, Op. Cit., p. 114.

6

Intuitive And Pragmatic

In the years leading up to World War II, as Adolf Hitler moved into power, a war weary British public did not want to listen to the warnings of Winston Churchill. Despite strong opposition, Churchill doggedly spoke out against the threat of a growing German war machine and the ugliness of Nazism.

As Hitler became more belligerent, British Prime Minister Neville Chamberlain flew to Germany to receive a promise of peace from the German leader. When Hitler proceeded to march on his neighbours, though, Chamberlain's dreams of peace were shattered. Shortly thereafter, he resigned and Churchill became Prime Minister – at the age of sixty-five. Winston wrote in his diary that the whole of his life and experience to that time had been a preparation for this moment and this one great task. His ultimate influence was slow in coming but when it arrived he was ready for it.

In that respect, he was similar to the prophet Daniel, but perhaps ever more so to Joseph. In Genesis 41, after languishing in an Egyptian prison, Joseph was suddenly brought to face-to-face with Pharaoh for the first time. The way the Bible relates it, he had time for nothing more than a shave and a change of clothes (Gen. 41:14-16). After 13 years of having his dreams trampled in the dust, he was finally presented with his one great chance to shine. Yet it seemed he'd had no time to prepare himself.

Actually, he'd been preparing for years. He may not have known how this moment would come, but he knew that it would. Like Daniel, he was ready for his time in the spotlight. He was armed with two things: revelation and an idea. The king, it turned out, was confused by a strange dream. In his big moment, Joseph quickly understood the content and the meaning of the king's dream. This came to him by divine revelation and it marked a new beginning for Joseph.

Revelation

The key characteristic of revelation is its speed. It can burst forth suddenly, in an instant, throwing light on everything it touches. Suddenly, you just 'know' something, though you can't be sure how the knowledge came to you.

We should never make the mistake, however, of thinking that its speed implies that revelation is accidental. Nor should we think that it is solely the result of God's sovereignty. The stories of Joseph and Daniel prove that the ability to receive revelation and appreciate it for what it is, are a product of desire, experience and practice. Over time, Joseph had become a man practiced in understanding revelation.

The church of 2020 will be skilled at receiving revelation and knowing how to apply it. It will be made up of Christians who have schooled themselves in revelation, without becoming 'super-spooks'. These people will be well taught in several disciplines.

Keeping A Relaxed Grip On Life

A recent study, conducted over several years, looked at why some people consider themselves to be lucky, and others do not. This survey asked the question: are there observable reasons why some people seem to attract better fortune than others? The results were very interesting.

Basically, said the study's author, there are certain characteristics that 'lucky' people seem to exhibit much more than 'unlucky' people. One of these is a relaxed and open attitude to life. People who feel they have good fortune seem to be able to see opportunities coming – because they're not so anxious or uptight as people who feel unfortunate.

These fortunate people tend to believe that good things will happen to them, that even when times are hard things will work out *for* them in the end. As a result, their eyes are always open to new opportunities, some of which spring right out of the blue.

God's promises are, in a sense, self-fulfilling prophecies. They re-set our expectations and fire our enthusiasm about ourselves. They alter our mood and therefore change the way we interact with the world around us. We become more open to new experiences and more attractive to others.

Golf can be the most frustrating game on the planet (unless you count curling as seen in the winter Olympics; it has to be the most frustrating to *watch*!). Golf coaches will tell you that you need to relax your grip just before you swing at the ball. Otherwise your muscles will tighten and you'll hit the ball every which way but straight.

Joseph had learned to play the 'game of life' with a relaxed grip. He'd discovered, by hard experience, that it's pointless and ultimately heart-breaking to try to predict God's next move. Joseph traveled light, ready to move at any moment, wherever providence would point him. Sometimes we don't see the opportunities around us because we are looking too hard for something else.

Philippians 4:6 says: 'Do not be anxious about anything, but in everything, by prayer and petition, with thanksgiving, present your requests to God.' If our prayer lives are filled only with asking for something, we can become obsessed and unable to see anything else. As soon as we add some thanksgiving to the mix, though, we relax our grip. Suddenly, we're seeing things from a higher perspective, taking in the big picture of what God has already done. That's when we're open to revelation.

Exercising Sanctified Intuition

Patrick Dixon, in the introduction to his book *'FutureWise'*, asks: 'What does third millennial life look like? [It is] faster, more technologically dominated; data obsessed but more intuitive, sensitive and environmentally aware.'[1] In the world of 2020, the desire to know will mix with the desire to sense. The world will respect people of intuition mixed with logic and wisdom combined with knowledge.

Deuteronomy 8:3 tells us that, 'man does not live on bread

[the things of the material or natural world] alone but on every word that comes from the mouth of the LORD.' Revelation sustains us in a way that reason cannot. It speaks through the soul, the intuitive part of our psyche.

Revelation comes first not to our logical faculties but to the part of our psyche where images are formed. We will *add* words to communicate what we know through revelation, but the revelation itself is not the child of rational processes; it comes from God. The imagination is very important, as that is where revelation first takes root. And imagination is, conversely, where so many of our problems begin!

This is why Paul tells us to use the spiritual weapons at our disposal to 'demolish arguments and every pretension [or, false imagination] that sets itself up against the knowledge of God...' (2 Cor. 10:4-5). We constantly engage our spiritual enemy in the battle of the mind, so as to protect the fortress of our imagination where revelation messages are received.

Maximizing 'Chance' Meetings

Sociologists have estimated that, on average, we all know approximately 300 people on a first name basis. Whenever we meet someone and start talking to them we are only one conversation away from the 300 other people whom *they* know. In turn, those 300 people each know another 300. Applying some basic maths, by meeting just one person, you are a handshake away from roughly 300 times 300, or 90,000 new possibilities!

Even in the prison house, where you'd expect Joseph to be sulking in a corner, he developed relationships and tried to maximize their potential. He invested time in the problems of the king's baker and butler, interpreting their dreams (Genesis 40:5-14). The butler later remembered Joseph just when it did the most good.[2]

Revelation is never spoken into a vacuum. God speaks to those who will act on what he says in response to human need. Revelation always seeks a practical outlet, because it is given to help us meet human needs.

A friend of mine, evangelist Arthur Blessitt, related to me a conversation he'd had with a one-time Texan oil millionaire. This businessman, who came from a prominent American family, sent friends to ask if Arthur could pray with him and introduce him to Christ. They met after one of Arthur's public meetings, in a private room backstage. Arthur prayed with this man, sensing that he was experiencing a revelation moment and making a heartfelt commitment to God.

For Arthur, this was just one of many hundreds of thousands of 'appointments' he's had around the world over a forty-year period. In most cases, he doesn't get to see the end result. This time, the result was clear. That oil executive was later elected President of the United States. Revelation moments often come on the back of what look like chance meetings.

Remaining Naturally Supernatural

God doesn't have to impress with way he talks: we can tell by the substance of what is said whether or not a message is from him. The church of 2020 will cultivate among its people the habit of being natural in the way they speak and live out revelation. It will teach that immediately revelation is received, it must look for a practical outlet, some benefit for others. Smith Wigglesworth observed that: 'We have the Acts of the Apostles because the apostles acted!'

All revelation must be measured against the compass of God's written word, which keeps us aligned with true north. The greatest Bible prophets, the people who received the greatest revelation, were students of the writings of earlier prophets. The church of 2020 will place great store on the Bible itself, building everything it does according to the measure of scripture.

What's The Big Idea?!

Joseph met his big opportunity for influence, his moment at court, with a revelation. Yet he was able to take things further even that that – because he married to that revelation a genius idea.

Revelation comes to the realm of the intuitive, but it must be lived out in the realm of the real. Revelation without application leads to stagnation. Insight without impact invites inertia. The church of 2020 will not be so pre-occupied with revelation that it can't generate practical ideas.

Ideas are the great motivators of change. I once spoke at a US conference alongside the legendary preacher T.L. Osborn. He defined leadership as 'people having good ideas'. Ideas are also the core of all good communication, which essentially brings people together around ideas.

Ideas are the things that drive history forward. Guttenberg's Bible, the first mass produced book, started with an idea. So did Bell's patent of the telephone, Edison's invention of the light bulb and Benz's first petrol driven car. The Wright brothers launched an idea long before they launched their first flight. Einstein revolutionised physics with an idea wrapped in a simple equation, $e=mc^2$.

Man's first landing on the moon, the launch of the World Wide Web and the mapping of the human genome all began as simple ideas. The church of 2020 will exercise influence because it trains its people to generate and work with ideas. Joseph came to his big moment with a big idea to match his big revelation.

Revelation and education are different. Revelation is built on enlightenment that originates outside of us. God initiates revelation. Ideas, on the other hand, are generated by our own thought processes, based in part on our education both formal and experience-based.

Yet revelation and education are not mutually exclusive events. It is possible to be a person of revelation and possess a keen and creative mind. In fact, we were created to learn and process information on two levels, through both revelation and education. Revelation processes information through the filter of God's kingdom, leading us to spiritual and moral truth above all. Education processes information through the filter of the natural world, leading us to truth about ourselves and our world.

All too often, Christians have felt pressured either to abandon education for revelation, or to shrug off revelation in favour of education. If the church has lost influence in the world, it's not primarily because of an increase in education, either in the church or the wider society. The problem is that we often don't want to submit education to revelation, or apply revelation through our education. So we are left with reason without revelation, leading to technology without truth.

In a truly enlightened mind, education is submitted to revelation and revelation is applied through education. The church of 2020 will have little problem generating potentially revolutionary ideas to match its potent revelation. It will train people not just to understand the spiritual realm of revelation, but to appreciate the intellectual realm of ideas.

Overcoming Mental Obesity

'To write about the past,' writes Edward de Bono, 'you only need some skill as a writer: the past is there to be described. To write about the future also needs some skill as a thinker.'[3] Having influence in the future requires an ability to think clearly. If we had more Christians who use their minds, I'm convinced we'd have more Christians!

Obesity is a huge threat to public health these days. Basically, it is usually the result of people consuming more calories than they can burn off in physical activity. In future, mental obesity will be just as big a problem, though it may not attract the same attention. This brand of obesity is a result of people consuming more *information* than they can 'burn off' in useful *mental* activity.

The average daily newspaper contains more information than most people would learn in a lifetime during the 1700s. The amount of information available to us will grow exponentially over the next decade. Why? Partly because of breakthroughs in new areas of research. We will see major breakthroughs coming in areas of science that are totally unknown today.

Our access to information will increase, too. Small, lightweight, hand-held devices will hold terabytes of information.

Information without useful application will increasingly lead to overload and confusion. When a disconnect occurs between what people are learning and what they can use, information becomes nothing but a burden. We need to discover how to discipline our own learning curves, discerning what we need to know and we most likely don't. We also need to become kinetic rather than passive learners, employing what we learn to better our lives and those of other people rather than simply storing it away on bookshelves (or, more likely, electronic book files).

In the midst of the information hike, we will also need to build our muscle in the area of original thinking. Some, like de Bono, have called this 'design thinking'. It involves more than processing someone else's ideas or shuffling around what's already known. It makes a deliberate habit of having innovative thoughts, ideas that make something out of nothing.

Original thinking does what it says on the pack – it thinks new thoughts! This is the only way we're going to be able to burn off excess information and save ourselves from overload.

A simple exercise to get you started: select from your newspaper or magazine one issue every week. Any issue on any major development. Then ask yourself a question: 'How does my Christian worldview respond to this issue or problem?' Don't answer with clichés or even just with proof texts from one part of the Bible. Try to see the witness of the whole of the Bible on that issue. It's a good way to start building your mental muscle.

Practice Makes Perfect

If, as some psychologists suggest, only a small percentage of our ideas are really useful, the more ideas we have the higher the likelihood that we'll come up with something revolutionary.

When it comes to ideas, quantity leads to quality. When was the last time you sat in a chair and asked God to help you have great ideas? When did you last have a personal brainstorming session? When did you last drive around for an hour just thinking through the thorny problems you face, letting your mind drift and settle on ideas?

The church of 2020 will promote and celebrate its thinkers, its idea-generators. People who come up with great ideas will become local heroes. In a world that will increasingly value knowledge and wisdom as much as money, the church will provide classes on how to produce and work with ideas, especially those that bring long-term change to society. It will offer skills for brainstorming, idea-selection, strategic thinking, the testing of ideas and the measurement of their success. In short, the church will produce people who are more into strategic thinking than mere wishful thinking!

Ideas That Pass The Test

Benjamin Franklin once remarked that, 'diligence is the mother of good luck.' That immortal philosopher, Oprah Winfrey, has said that, 'luck is a matter of preparation meeting opportunity.'

Joseph had seven years to wait until his prophecy would be fulfilled. Seven years to think about what the consequences might be if he was wrong. During those seven years he taxed the Egyptians heavily, storing up crops for the coming drought. He must have thought, 'What will they do to him if the drought never comes? What if the seven good years are followed by seven even *better* years?'

It's relatively painless to offer ideas within the safety of the church family. Your brothers and sisters care about you. Even if they don't agree with your ideas, they'll try to couch their rejection in the nicest and most affirming words. Outside the church door, though, things are different – people won't tell you what you want to hear. They'll say emphatically whether or not they like what you're putting forward.

But the call to influence demands that you take the risk. Joseph allowed his ideas to be subjected to trial, putting his neck on the line to test them. The church of 2020 will take the same risk.

THE CHURCH OF 2020

Can We Get A Little Service Here?

'Life is an exciting business,' wrote Helen Keller, 'and most exciting when lived for others.' In the age of Big Brother and its siblings in the Reality-TV family, service is giving way to selfishness. Process-thinking is being replaced by event-addiction. People like to see themselves as the centre of an event, rather than a part of a longer process. This is why so many people burn out: they think the entire story starts and ends with them. They have no proper sense of perspective.

John Wesley prayed, 'Let me not live to be useless.' Today, we cry, 'Let me not live to be nameless!' Everybody wants their 15 minutes of fame as if that is a birthright. But what happens when you get to minute number twenty – is life all downhill from there? And what if you never get your 15 minutes in the spotlight – has your life been a waste of time?

The ideas that produce the most change will always come to those who put their lives on the line; those who serve something bigger than themselves, something that will live on when they die. In the church of 2020, this will not be unusual.

---

1 'FutureWise', Patrick Dixon (Profile books, 2004), introduction.
2 For more on this, see 'The Joseph Chronicles', Mal Fletcher, (Next Wave International, 1998, 2003).
3 'New Thinking for the New Millenium', Edward de Bono, (Penguin Books, 2000), p. 112.

7

From Cinema To City Council

In the first chapter of the Bible, God lays out his first mandate for humankind. They must, he says, influence and shape their world (Genesis 1:26-28). The first calling God gave us was to impact our world more than it impacts us. Influence is hardwired into the human condition. One way or the other, influence will flow.

All around us everyday, there is a battle for influence going on. Light against darkness, flesh versus spirit, temporal versus eternal and spin against truth. We have a choice to make: either we will influence the often egocentric culture around us or it will most certainly force us into its mould (cf. Romans 12:2).

Either we will invent the future or someone else's vision of the future will re-invent us.

When Mel Gibson's 'The Passion of the Christ' first hit the big screen, it caused controversy partly because people are not used to being confronted with Christian truth in the realm of mainstream art and thought. People are often more familiar with Christians who live in a cultural bubble and church leaders who speak only to the converted. Some are more comfortable with a Christianity like that – because they can dismiss it out of hand.

It's not easy for people to adjust to hearing from Christians who push the boundaries of creative achievement or expression.

The church of 2020 will do just that. It will challenge the idea that the church is just a small group operating on the periphery of mainstream culture. It will boldly go where the church has seldom gone before in modern times – into a full-on engagement with every area of the popular culture, from the cinema to the city council.

Village Vs. Market

For centuries, people lived predominantly in small towns or villages where they spent most of their lives. They seldom worked or travelled outside the village of their birth. In the traditional village, the community was largely self-sufficient. What it could not supply for itself, using the skills, materials and services available within it, it either did without or imported once a week on market day.

Market day was a big event. It was marked by lots of noise, colour and merchants arriving from out of town, hungry to compete for the attention of the local clientele. The market was dependant on the village; it fed off the buzz of village life.

Today, the situation is reversed. Long an adjunct to the town, the market has now swallowed the town whole! People no longer look just within their geographical locale to find services, products and resources. They drive miles to find what they need or, increasingly, go online to search an area much wider than their own hometown. People do this to find friendships, too. Instead of the market being part of the town or reliant on the town, the town is part of the market and reliant on the market.

The market has now swallowed the town whole.

In recent times, the church has sometimes missed its full potential influence because it is too 'local' for its own good! It has often concentrated on the town to the exclusion of the marketplace. As a result, it has allowed itself to be shut out of the spheres of influence that impact daily on people's lives – such as media, the entertainment industry, politics and so on.

Local And Beyond

The church of 2020 *will* focus on building local church, but with a view to extending the global Kingdom of God. What is the Kingdom of God? I've written on this more extensively elsewhere, but basically the Kingdom is where the love and rule of Christ are transforming human hearts, relationships and institutions.[1]

The Kingdom is wherever God's will is done on earth as it is in heaven – that is, out of love, not fear and with an emphasis on justice, mercy and humility (Micah 6:8). It is wherever people of changed hearts go on to change their world.

The Kingdom was Jesus' first priority. He mentioned the Kingdom more than 100 times in the gospels, while using the Greek word for church – ecclesia – on just three occasions. Does this mean the local church is not important to Jesus? Certainly not – the rest of the New Testament is all about the establishment of local churches. Jesus wanted our priorities to be right, that's all. 'Seek first the Kingdom of God and his righteousness,' he taught, 'and all these things will be added to you.' The church of 2020 will grow because it will seek first the growth of the Kingdom.

An entire local church can't normally be present in one place of business, but the Kingdom can. A local church can't be present in an entertainment factory – a movie studio for example – but the Kingdom can. The church of 2020 will equip its people to carry true Kingdom values wherever they go. The church of 2020 will not be so 'local' that it can't see the bigger picture. It will not suffer from 'village thinking'. It will build locally, yes, but it will definitely plan and act on a much bigger scale. It will think as did the apostle Paul.

Paul, The Strategist

In Acts 16, Paul took Jesus' message for the first time into Western Europe. What started as a very small seed has grown into a huge tree of witness and influence that has re-shaped much of the world. Paul was a strategic thinker. We know that, yet we often miss one half of his strategy. Paul seems to have had a two-pronged approach in his outreach.

First, Paul targeted cities; urban centres that would give the quickest spread to the gospel. Paul knew that urban centres don't simply reflect the culture of a nation, they actively shape it. If you can touch a city, you can touch a nation. The city is where the national myth is enshrined, where you find the core expressions of the culture and values of a nation. Especially today, where major cities form the epicentre of communications media, arts and technological development. John Dawson has written that 'a nation is the sum of its cities.'

In Paul's day, Thessalonica was the capital of Macedonia, and the centre of its culture. Corinth was a major commercial centre with a double harbour. Athens was the cultural centre of Achaia, or Greece, and it exerted a great influence on the whole Roman world. Cities allowed Paul to build churches which would then serve as models for their surrounding regions.

There has always been something attractive about living in a major city, close to the action, near the heart of the culture. Governments in many nations are trying to feed this human passion for cities in a controlled fashion using new city design. One architect has been commissioned by the Chinese government to build seven new cities for 400 million people by 2017.

Today, globalisation promises work in urban centres, yet cities often struggle to keep up with the growth. In today's world, more than 70 million people a year migrate from the country to cities, or 130 every minute, according to one expert. Many of these people set up home in squats which are built from scarce materials. In 2005, there were one billion squatters in the world; by 2050, that figure will reach three billion. In the West, we will see the development of shanty-towns inside major urban enclaves, with a very clear delineation between the affluent and the poor parts of cities.

Some authorities are now warning of dramatic summer heat waves in many previously cooler cities of the world. The level of CO_2 in the atmosphere has risen by 30 percent in the past 200 years of industrialisation. In the last century, the worldwide average temperature rose by about 0.6 degrees Celsius – and in Europe by about one degree. This is set to increase, say many scientists.

More intense summers will result. People will turn to air-conditioning to deal with the heat, consuming more power resources and releasing even more greenhouse gases. More people in our cities will struggle for the basics of life such as water, power and even food. They will face serious health risks resulting from pollution and resource-depletion.

Yet people will continue to gravitate toward major urban centres, both old and new, in the hope of finding a richer and better life. Cities will continue to offer great promise for 'winners' and great pain for life's 'losers'. These cities will need strong churches – thousands of them. They will need churches that are as focussed on providing material services and emotional support as they are on meeting spiritual needs.

New Churches, New Markets

Once again in our time, God is sending an army of church planters into cities and mega-cities. Once again, we are learning to focus energies and resources on population centres. The church of 2020 will see much more of this. In the face of often fierce opposition and even persecution, pioneer leaders will embark on bold and often aggressive church-planting strategies that will shake cities in the way the early apostles often did. Persecution will only serve to make their witness and faith stronger. Miracles will be commonplace, especially where Christianity is most maligned.

Fledgling churches will form alliances with larger and more resourceful churches who will act as their sponsors. Churches will no longer link up because of denominational ties – this is breaking down even now – but because of a passionate desire to impact a certain region in a certain way. New churches will also be born among sub-cultures. Tribalism will grow in society in answer to globalisation. New churches will build on people's desire to link up with others who share a common cultural heritage or social values.

Generational churches will be much more common, too. You can expect to see the birth of the first mega-churches made up mainly of children, or of teens and young adults. Some church planters will work at the other end of the age scale. Generational churches will arise, specifically aiming to reach ageing Baby Boomers and/or retiring Gen-Xers.

Traditional churches will form strong functional ties with very avant-garde, cutting-edge groups. Recently, I spoke in a large, 600 year-old church building in England. The building was something like a cathedral but the service was run by a church that's less than two years old. Old stones rocked that night! Many young adults came to faith in Christ and the church received great press coverage. This will become much more widespread as churches put aside doctrinal or historic differences to meet the harsh challenges posed by humanism, existentialism and the aggressive growth of other faiths.

The church of 2020 will be more strategic than we are at present. Churches will not simply *tolerate* the planting of new works in their own backyard; they will deliberately pursue it. One major church for even a small city or town will no longer be acceptable. Churches will grow even when they're in close proximity to each other, as local people react to increasing social alienation, seeking community built around the greatest cause of all.

Some mega-churches will continue to attract large numbers of people and will provide an invaluable showcase of what the church can achieve. The most successful of these will invest hugely in resourcing Christian witness the world over.

In some urban centres, mega-churches will cease to pay over-inflated prices for property, instead meeting in theatres and large industrial complexes. Some will, as one writer put it, get over their 'edifice complex' realising that while grand buildings do sometimes honour God, risky living does it better. My home church in London is only a few years old, but already has more than 6000 people associated with it. Meetings are held in major theatres in and around the city of London. Buildings, though, are seen simply as containers for people.

Some suburban mega-churches will suffer, though, as fuel shortages and/or changeovers to alternative fuels bite into the driving culture. And some mega-churches will go the way of the dinosaur because they have not built generationally or have relied too much on the life and ministry of an individual leader. Sadly, in some places huge church buildings will stand like the empty cathedrals of today, until someone comes to revitalise faith in their communities.

Meanwhile, grassroots church life will flourish – where so-called 'Body ministry' will function under effective visionary leadership. By 2020, Baby Boomers will seek a final opportunity to 'live the dream' of their youth and change the world. Gen-Xers will have time and money on their hands and will bring their more pragmatic worldview to help churches produce hard results on the ground.

Millennials will be at their prime in terms of influence. Those who were reached for Christ in their youth will continue to serve, helping to build institutions and services for the good of society. Their less individualistic, more team-based approach, combined with the sheer size of their generation, will push the church even further away from narrow sectarian concerns and in the direction of a lasting social legacy. You can also expect to see a huge intake of Millennials as many in their twenties and thirties come to hear the gospel for the first time in their lives.

Spheres Of Influence

Paul targeted major cities, but there was another strand to his strategy. He also seems to have focussed on spheres of influence, areas of thought and practice which shape the thinking of people and strongly impact their everyday lives. Among the Paul's very first converts in Europe were people who would represent major spheres of influence even in today's world.

Lydia, the first European brought to faith by Paul, was an international trader in valuable goods, a woman of commerce (Acts 16:14). The second was the Philippian jailer (Acts 16:34). He was more than a prison guard; he was a civil servant, a steward of the legal system, a kind of bureaucrat.

Then Paul debated and shared with the members of the Athenian Aerapogas who met on Mars Hill (Acts 17:18-20). Among them were philosophers, academics, educators and sponsors of the arts. I once stood on this historic spot and felt moved as I recalled the profound yet simple presentation Paul made to these leading thinkers. After this, Paul reached out to Dionysius. He was a member of the city council, a politician (Acts 17:34).

We also read that other community leaders were converted in those early days, including wives of leading men and other prominent women (Acts 17:4).

For many centuries since the time of Paul, Europe was the home of Christian faith, the birthplace of every major Christian denomination. T. R. Reid writes: 'For nearly 1500 years, Europe was more or less synonymous with Christendom... Europe was a devoutly Christian place, and the global centre of the Christian faith.'[2]

Today, Europe is a much less religious place. Historian Norman Davies, writing in the 1990s, said that 'for the first time in 1500 years, Christianity [has become] a minority religion' in Europe. At least one major international news magazine has dubbed Europe the darkest place in the world, spiritually speaking. A Dutch sociologist called Europe's one of the least religious populations in the world.

That may be true, but I have lived in two European capitals over the past ten years and worked in most of the others. I can tell you from experience that a new type of church is emerging on this continent; two new generations of Christians are arising who have a passion to reshape the spiritual priorities of their common European home. It will take time to change attitudes to faith in what is very much a secularised region, but God loves to do things where people say they can't be done!

For all Europe's seeming abandonment of religious faith, however, Christian values still pervade its culture. Through those values Europe impacts the world in just about every other sphere of life. Reid says:

> *'[Europe] covers just six percent of the earth's total area and is home to just 12 percent of the global population. Yet Europe has 40 percent of the world's wealth and accounts for more than half of all global commerce.*

European countries comprise five of the world's ten richest nations.'

'The continent was the birthplace of "Western values," the combination of individual rights, democratic governments, and free markets that has spread around the world... European art, music, architecture, literature and legal concepts have been copied everywhere, with local variations. The increasingly common language of the continent, English, has spread from its small island birthplace to become the second most widely spoken language on earth (after Chinese).'[3]

What are the areas in which Western European thought and practice have most influenced the world since the first century? Commerce is certainly one. Western practices have shaped the world of international trade and are now at the forefront of the process of globalisation. Another is law and bureaucracy. Western systems of law enforcement and jurisprudence have been the benchmark for justice across much of the world. Western-style systems of bureaucracy also shape the administration of many governments the world over, for better or for worse.

Western – and European – influence can also be seen the world over in the arts and education. Western thinking has contributed much to the arts world – from the time of Aristotle and Plato. The most revered galleries are still to be found in the West. So are many of the world's most prestigious universities.

Then there's politics. Western liberal democracy has been accepted as a political ideal in much of the developed world. Even repressive regimes are opening their doors to contact with democracies because they see the benefits, at least financially if not morally and politically.

Sowing Into The Spheres

Through Paul, God ensured that the seeds of the gospel were sown into the key areas where Western influence would later shape world thought and behaviour.

The church of 2020 will treat this kind of approach as a foundation principle. It will proactively involve itself in every major sphere of influence within its city. In particular, it will target the one or two spheres for which the city is best known.

This church will, for example, employ its own 'company evangelists' who will work from the church into the business culture. Gen-Xers in particular will shift career-paths – not jobs within the same industry – six or seven times over their working lives. The church of 2020 will strike up arrangements with major companies for the release of business chaplains, who will offer counsel and support for people making those transitions. Some companies will actually seek out the church's help in providing spiritual support at crucial times in their workers' lives.

Denis Waitley has written that knowledge is the frontier of tomorrow.[4] Peter Drucker, the management expert, says that knowledge has power, controlling access to opportunity and advancement.[5] These days, you don't need money to make money – you need knowledge. This trend is set to continue.

In many areas, university and college virtual campuses will attract far more people than traditional bricks and mortar institutions. This trend is already in place, but is set to increase. Lectures, notes, tutors and tutorial group sessions will all be accessed via a very souped-up version of the Internet. Texts will be available in many formats, but perhaps the most popular will be those featuring digitally 'printed' text on plasma-screen 'pages'. Hard copy, DIY 'print-at-point-of-delivery' books will also be an option for those who prefer the feel of traditional books on recycled or synthetic paper.

Church With No Walls

The church of 2020 will have a real presence in the world of education and the development of ideas. New universities will be founded by Christian benefactors and churches, aligned with local congregations or church networks. Rather than seeing this as a diversion from the true work of the church, many Christians will see this as the only way to regain a foothold for Christian thought in an aggressively pluralistic society.

The church of 2020 will also engage with the world of civic leadership and governance as a natural extension of its Kingdom priority. It will do this without becoming party political. It will openly encourage its members to speak up on issues that concern them, guided by the word of God and individual conscience. It will also place itself at the service of prominent civic leaders, offering prayer and a witness for righteousness. Political figures are human beings first and this church will treat them as such.

Each year my wife Davina and I host a meeting of European church network leaders. The Strategic Leadership Consultation brings together like-minded leaders of major church and ministry networks, for a summit on changing Europe's future through the gospel. In 2005, our meeting in London focussed on how the church can build bridges of trust and influence with civic leaders. At the end of the summit we published a Statement of Intent which was released to the press. The statement outlined a commitment and a roadmap for future action. This roadmap can be applied to church work in all spheres of influence in a community, not just the political. It's a great guide for leaders who want to touch the marketplace:

As leaders of European church networks / ministries, we affirm that we will:

i. Build churches and ministries that look to shape the future of cities today.

ii. Work to create a better future for all the people in our cities and communities.

iii. Build churches and ministries which, if they were not present, would be missed by their communities.

iv. Encourage in Christian leaders a passion to bless the city and not just the church and to provide leadership for the city.

v. Pray for those in government and civic leadership.

vi.   Help political leaders to find pragmatic solutions to community problems.

vii.   Develop agendas of care for our cities and towns, promoting acts of kindness.

viii.   Promote what we stand for in the community, not simply what we stand against.

ix.   Bring people together, building inclusive alliances to solve community problems, while maintaining the core elements of our faith.

x.   Develop leaders who are as comfortable in the community as they are in the church.

xi.   Work to gain the trust of politicians and other civic leaders, by establishing a positive track record for solving problems.

xii.   Equip and support people from within our churches who are called to work in the political sphere.

xiii.   Offer a voice of moral conscience for our cities and nations – in a positive, respectful and engaging way.

xiv.   Pursue constructive influence, through intimacy (with God) alongside involvement (with the community).

Everything Is Mission, Mission Is Everything

The church of 2020 will treat engagement in the spheres of influence as it does world mission. In fact, reaching the worlds of business, education, politics, media and so on will feature in mission programs alongside preaching on foreign fields. Special ministers will be trained for each of the areas chosen for mission.

Bible training schools – both local and regional – will offer specialist training for business pastors, media pastors, chaplains to the entertainment world and so on. As with all other areas of mission, people who do not work fulltime in the field will be encouraged to send others in their place, through their giving.

The church of 2020 will not need to make a choice between targeting geographical areas or spheres of influence. It will do both at once.

---

[1] For more on this see 'The Pioneer Spirit', Mal Fletcher, (Authentic Media, 2002).
[2] 'The United States of Europe', T. R. Reid (Penguin books, 2004), p. 214
[3] Ibid., p. 245.
[4] 'Seeds of Greatness', Denis Waitley, (Revell Publishing, 1983), p. 88
[5] Ibid.

Other Books by Mal Fletcher

Youth: The Endangered Species

Get Real!

Burning Questions

Making God Famous

The Pioneer Spirit

The Joseph Chronicles

Youth Outreach Events

The Future is X

These titles are available at:

www.malfletcher.com

Watch for new titles announced at this site.

YOU

CAN HELP MAL FLETCHER AND HIS TEAM
Make a Permanent Impact on Europe!

SOW A SEED INTO GOOD SOIL

www.nextwaveonline.com